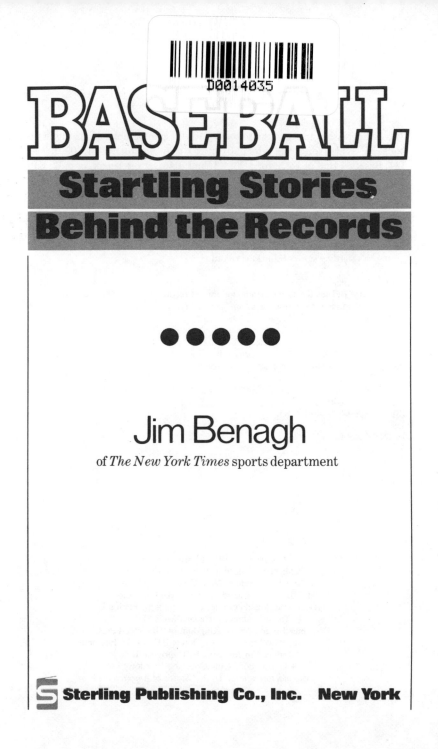

BASEBALL

Startling Stories
Behind the Records

• • • • •

Jim Benagh

of *The New York Times* sports department

Sterling Publishing Co., Inc.   New York

The author wishes to thank the following for the photographs appearing in this book: AP/Wide World Photos for p 10 (Pruett), p 76 (Squires), p 101, 102, 109 and 124; Baseball Hall of Fame for p 23, 83, and 104; Detroit Tigers for p 37; UPI/Bettmann Newsphotos for p 15 and 85; Jerry Wachter and the Baltimore Orioles for p 67; and Dale Long himself for p 76.

Library of Congress Cataloging-in-Publication Data

Benagh, Jim, 1937–
  Baseball startling stories behind the records.

  Includes index.
  Summary: Relates the stories behind number of record-setting feats in the history of baseball, in such categories as "Long-ball Sluggers," "Age Gaps," and Hitting Feats."
    1. Baseball—United States—Records—Juvenile literature. 2. Baseball—United States—Juvenile literature. [1. Baseball—Records. 2. Baseball—History] I. Title.
GV877.B39 1987   796.357'0973'021   86-30137
ISBN 0-8069-6402-2
ISBN 0-8069-6403-0 (lib. bdg.)

ISBN 0-8069-6788-9 (pbk.)

5   7   9   10   8   6   4

Copyright © 1987 by Jim Benagh
Published by Sterling Publishing Co., Inc.
Two Park Avenue, New York, N.Y. 10016
Distributed in Canada by Oak Tree Press Ltd.
% Canadian Manda Group, P.O. Box 920, Station U
Toronto, Ontario, Canada M8Z 5P9
Distributed in the United Kingdom by Blandford Press
Link House, West Street, Poole, Dorset BH15 1LL, England
Distributed in Australia by Capricorn Ltd.
P.O. Box 665, Lane Cove, NSW 2066
Manufactured in the United States of America

Contents

• I •
Men with Golden Arms

Clemens' Phenomenal Comeback

When Dwight Gooden of the New York Mets won 24 games and lost only four in the 1985 season, baseball experts thought they were watching the second coming of Sandy Koufax, who had left the game almost two decades before. Here was a young pitcher with all the speed and control to reign as the big leagues' top pitcher for years. After all, only eight pitchers in the previous half century, Koufax included, had won 20 more games than they lost in a single season. Moreover, Gooden, at just 21 years old, had the stuff to surpass that startling record of 19 strikeouts in a game, shared by Steve Carlton, Tom Seaver and Nolan Ryan, all headed for the Hall of Fame.

While Gooden became America's most popular coverboy, Roger Clemens of the Boston Red Sox was concerned as to whether his once-promising career was at an end. He had undergone shoulder surgery in August

1985 after being on the disabled list twice. The 23-year-old right-handed Texan, thinking each may be his last trip to the mound in the majors, was in tears.

In 1986, however, a year in which Gooden found it difficult to match his previous performance, Clemens took over as baseball's No. 1 pitcher. Many of his statistics closely matched Gooden's 1985 marks.

But Clemens added one extra twist.

It came on April 29, before a small crowd of 13,414 at Fenway Park in Boston. Most of the city's sports fans, long used to their Red Sox' failures, were over at Boston Garden or at their television sets watching the Celtics on their way to another world title in basketball.

The big Texan, still baby-faced despite his 220 pounds, began mowing down the Seattle Mariners, a pretty good-hitting team. Clemens' control was remarkable throughout the game as he only gave the Mariners 10 pitches that they could put into play and he didn't walk a man. He was regaining the confidence and control that had made him the star of the University of Texas' collegiate national champions and a standout in the Boston farm system.

In previous starts in 1986, he won each time, but only recorded two, seven and 10 strikeouts, respectively.

This game was a different story.

He struck out the side in the first inning, got two more in the second and one in the third. Spike Owen of the Mariners put an end to Clemens' no-hitter leading off the fourth with a single. But the pitcher responded by striking out the side again. He fanned all three men in the next inning, and the first two in the sixth—making eight strikeouts in a row.

With two more in the seventh, he brought his total to 16 and the record was in sight.

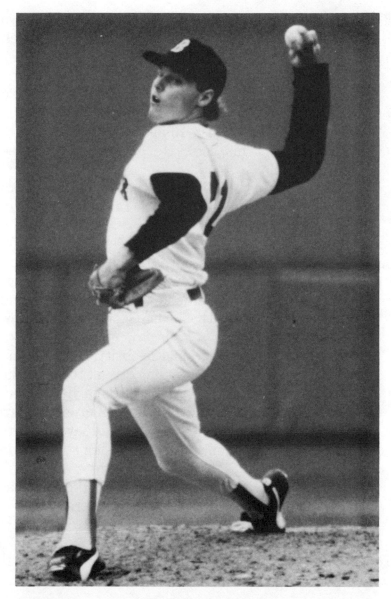

Roger Clemens of the Red Sox matched or surpassed some pretty famous pitchers in 1986 by striking out 20 batters in one game early in the year.

It would now be a test of his stamina. He added two more in the eighth inning and then, as he admitted later, he began "throwing on adrenaline."

A teammate reminded him that he was just one strikeout away from tying the nine-inning game record (another pitcher, Tom Cheney of the Old Washington Senators, once had 21 in a 16-inning game).

Clemens kept his cool. He got Owen on three straight fastballs.

Fenway was in bedlam. Even the Mariners went to the steps of the dugout to watch in appreciation of history being made.

The next batter, Phil Bradley, seemed justifiably nervous. Clemens, in the groove that pitchers crave for, gave him the one-two-three treatment, too. The last batter grounded out, but Clemens walked off the mound with a piece of history that even Gooden would have been proud of.

Clemens was now a national celebrity. But he didn't stop being one. He ran his winning streak to 14 by the end of June, and in the July All-Star Game, he started, and put down nine National Leaguers in order to earn the victory as well as the Most Valuable Player award. A touch of irony: Gooden was the opposing starter and took the loss.

Clemens went on to a 24–4 record, the same as Gooden had finished with the season before.

Pitcher Masters Babe Ruth

Baseball has a term for a pitcher who's got a batter's number. It's called a "collar."

Babe Ruth, the remarkable slugger of the New York Yankees, rarely was stopped repeatedly by any pitcher during his dazzling 22-year career—and if he was, it wasn't for long. A .342 lifetime hitter with those famous 714 home runs, Ruth could hit his way out of any adverse situation.

But one season Ruth was collared by a pitcher. It happened in 1922. Babe's conqueror turned out to be a 21-year-old rookie with the nickname "Shucks."

Hub (Shucks) Pruett was a little 165-pounder for the St. Louis Browns, who were to give the Yankees a run for the American League pennant in 1922. Baseball was secondary to Pruett. A graduate of the University of Missouri, he was more intent on working his way through medical school than collaring future Hall of Famers.

Pruett wasn't any more awed by his own baseball talents than he was by those of famous sluggers like Ruth. As a youth, his sandlot friends made him pitch because he couldn't throw straight from other positions. At the University of Missouri, he had a little curve and a screwball and not much more. "I didn't think I could fool major leaguers," he said years later. But he needed the money, so he tried.

What Hub Pruett did to Ruth in 1922 has grown in legend over the years. The *Sporting News*, baseball's generally reliable "bible," once ran a not-quite-true article about Pruett fanning Ruth 13 straight times and giving him only one hit in 19 times at bat during the heated pennant race between St. Louis and the Yankees

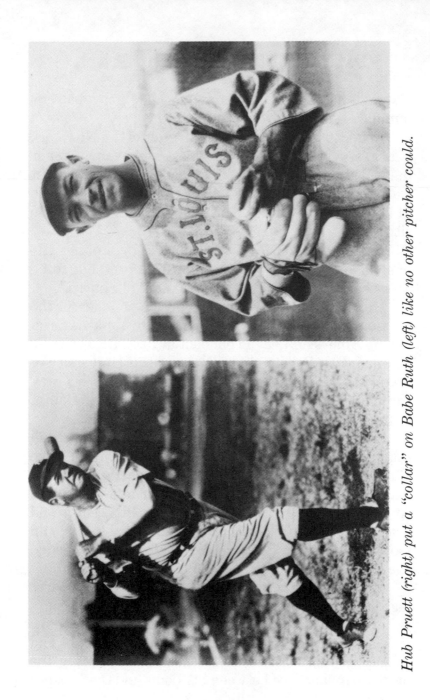

Hub Pruett (right) put a "collar" on Babe Ruth (left) like no other pitcher could.

in 1922. That would have been a startling accomplishment for a pitcher who posted only a 7-7 record for his first big-league season.

Pruett wasn't that good, but he was good enough.

Between May and September, 1922, Shucks Pruett struck out Ruth 10 times in the 16 times the mighty Yankee confronted him. Since Pruett walked Ruth three times, that was 10 "K's" in 13 official at-bats.

Of the first 12 times Ruth swung against the Brown upstart, over a course of five games, the Babe struck out nine times and once grounded out meekly to the pitcher. The ground-out in the fourth game was the closest Ruth had come to getting a piece of the ball in four months against his young nemesis. In two other plate appearances, Pruett walked Ruth.

Here's how Pruett did it:

May 22: In a four-inning relief stint, Pruett struck out Ruth once and walked him once. Ruth had homered against the Browns earlier in the game.

June 10: Again in relief, Pruett fanned Ruth the only time they faced each other.

June 12: Making his first start against the Yankees, Pruett struck out Ruth three times and walked him once—and got credit for winning the game, though he lasted only six innings.

July 12: Again, Pruett set Ruth down swinging three times and got him the last time with the bases loaded to preserve a 7-4 victory for the Browns. In another confrontation that day, Ruth got a piece of the ball and dribbled it back to Pruett for an infield out.

August 25: Pruett was still suffering from a sore arm that had cost him an opportunity to meet Ruth for a second time in July. But when the Babe came to bat with the bases loaded, he pitched anyway and, naturally, struck him out.

September 17: By now, the pennant race was hot and the fans were siding with the amazing rookie phenom who had struck out Ruth in nine of 10 official at-bats. Pruett revved up that crowd even more when, after walking Ruth in the first inning, he struck him out in the third. Ruth finally broke the spell in the fifth inning with one of his towering homeruns. Later in the game, which the Browns won by a 5-1 score, Ruth also singled. They didn't meet again until 1923.

For the season, Ruth had batted only .158 against a good, though hardly sensational, rookie. A man who homered in one out of every 8.5 at-bats during his fabled career managed just one homer in 13 at-bats against a heretofore unknown.

Ruth hit only .315 and 35 homers in 1922—well below his usual norms. But that should not detract from Pruett's accomplishments.

The following season, when Ruth got back into the groove (batting .393 and smacking a league-leading 41 homers), Pruett again began to harass him. Pruett struck him out three times in their first meeting, though he gave up a walk and a homer in the same contest.

Thus Pruett brought his remarkable string to 13 strikeouts in 17 official at-bats by Ruth.

Shucks Pruett was often asked how a raw rookie like himself could "collar" the most famous slugger in baseball history. He said he had no secret and didn't pitch any differently than he did to other players, who gave him more than his share of problems. He had a left-handed version of Christy Mathewson's strange fadeaway pitch, and that was the particular pitch that befuddled Ruth in crucial situations. It fell away from the plate when it neared the homerun-record slugger.

"I suppose I just didn't have the mental hazard,"

Pruett mused in later years. "I suppose the reason was that I wasn't a rabid fan as a kid. Big names didn't mean much to me. I just wanted to be a doctor."

Pruett made a name for himself in baseball history that first season. Though he was no raving success, except against Ruth, he did strike out 70 men in slightly less than 120 innings and was a good enough hurler to help the Browns make a run for the 1922 pennant.

After his first matchup with Ruth in 1923, however, he held no more spell over the Babe and struck him out only one more time. For 1923 and 1924, Pruett won only seven games for the Browns and was phased out of the American League. He managed to get four more seasons of play in the National League between 1927 and 1932, then retired from the game with a mediocre 29-48 record.

But during his undistinguished major-league career, he earned his medical degree, and became a practicing physician in St. Louis. He wasn't a bragger, but he liked to talk about the old days when Babe Ruth put him through medical school. It was a kindness Ruth gave to no other pitcher during his famed career.

Right-Hander Strikes Out 27 Batters in a Game

To strike out five of six batters is an accomplishment that any pitcher would like. But to strike out five of *every* six men you face is something pitchers don't even bother to fantasize about.

Yet one man achieved that feat—and a lot of other strikeout feats—during his short stay during the 1952 season in the minor leagues.

Until May 13 of that year, Ron Necciai's name was known only for its difficult pronunciation (*Netch*-eye)— and known only within the vast Pittsburgh Pirate farm system. The Pirates' brilliant general manager, Branch Rickey, had tried to launch the reorganization of the downtrodden Pirates by rounding up as many strong-armed American youths as he could. Rickey was dealing in numbers; Necciai, a 19-year-old ex-football star from Monongahela, Pa., was just one of them.

Necciai was shipped out to the Appalachian League team of Bristol, which represented the twin cities of that name in Virginia and Tennessee. Bristol was Class D baseball, as low as you can get, but a good starting point for unseasoned teenagers just out of high school.

When Necciai reported, he found himself among a lot of strong arms that the Rickey network had discovered. Among his teammates were pitchers named Bill Bell (who would record 194 strikeouts in 112 innings that year) and Frank Ramsey (180 strikeouts in 194 innings).

After a couple of warmup games, however, none of the fastball pitchers could match Necciai.

A crowd of 1,853 gathered at Bristol, Va., on May 13 to watch the local team play Welch, W. Va., in a regular-season contest. What they saw was beyond belief.

Necciai, a sturdy right-hander, struck out the side in the first inning. He struck out the first man to face him in the second. Then the Welch team's leftfielder got a piece of the ball but grounded out, shortstop to first base. Necciai fanned the last batter of the inning.

And the next three.

And the next three.

And so on.

Ron Necciai's strikeout records may never be broken.

Going into the ninth inning, the amazing left-hander had struck out 23 batters. Only that ground-ball out in the second inning prevented him from recording 24 out of a possible 24 strikeouts in the first eight innings.

In the top of the ninth inning, Necciai struck out the first two batters to bring his game total now to 25—matching the all-time organized (professional) baseball record for one game. And he had one more batter to face.

Along with his startling strikeout string, Necciai had a no-hit game going. The only batters who had reached base were one whom Necciai had hit with a pitch and another he had walked. Most of his teammates could have taken the night off. But not the catcher.

Behind the plate that night was Harry Dunlop, who was earning his salary that season trying to control Branch Rickey's whiff kids. He had done a marvelous job handling Necciai throughout the first eight innings.

But with two outs in the ninth, Dunlop dropped a third strike. Before he could recover the ball, Welch's speedy centerfielder Bobby Hammond scampered to first base.

By baseball scoring rules, the pitcher gets credit for a strikeout if the catcher muffs the third strike. The catcher is given an error for dropping the ball.

That made 26 for the night—a startling performance. That's just what Necciai had as he took the mound to face another Welch batter.

He then proceeded to strike out one more!—and bring his total to 27—a record no one has come close to matching in professional baseball.

Almost as impressive was the fact that 10 of those opponents had watched Necciai's fastball whiz by them without taking the bats off their shoulders. He was that fast that night.

Necciai naturally became the talk of the baseball world right after his astounding performance. Branch Rickey dispatched his son, Branch Jr., to Bristol to keep an eye on the arm. National League President Warren Giles wired Necciai to tell him, "I hope it won't be long before you're striking out American League batters in the All-Star Game." And potential ticket buyers in the little minor-league community anxiously awaited Necciai's next start.

Was his performance a fluke?

Hardly.

Necciai didn't start again until May 21, eight nights later. But against the Kingsport, Tenn. team, he fanned a grand total of 24 batters in a nine-inning game. A crowd of more than 5,000 cheered him on.

In his next two starts, Necciai continued to daze the youthful opponents who made up Class D rosters. He recorded 20 and then 19 strikeouts. That brought his total to 90 in four full games. Combined with the strikeouts he had in parts of two other games for Bristol, Necciai now had a total of 109 strikeouts in 42⅔ innings. In addition, he had a 4-0 record, and had given up only two earned runs during his stay at Bristol. His control had been pretty good, too; his slate showed only 20 walks and 10 hits in that span. He was not yet 20 years old.

Meanwhile, he had made believers out of Rickey and Co. The Pirates advanced Necciai to their Burlington (North Carolina) team for a brief stay in better competition—and then up to the majors at the end of the season.

Necciai didn't awe the big leaguers with his fastball. But the Pirates were a miserable last-place team, 54½ games behind the league leaders, and they offered little support for a young pitcher just off the sandlots of nearby Monongahela. Necciai pitched 54⅔ innings in 12 games that year and struck out 31 batters. He won one of seven decisions.

Ulcers, a sore arm and other physical problems caused by the strain on his lanky 6-foot-5-inch, 185-pound body curtailed Necciai's development. He toiled in the minors for some time after 1952, then faded out of the baseball picture. He never did reach the majors again.

*   *   *

Almost as astounding is the fact that Necciai's teammate, Bill Bell, was also a strikeout whiz, and so was the same team's Frank Ramsey. During the month of May that year, Bell teamed with Necciai to perform perhaps the most unusual series of games ever staged by two minor-league pitchers. On May 13, Necciai had his 27-strikeout no-hitter. Then on May 22, Bell went out and pitched a no-hitter against Kingsport only one night after Necciai had fanned 24 of the Kingsport batters.

It was strange as no-hitters go, because Bell let 11 batters get on base via walks. Two others got on base via errors. Still, Bell hung in there, striking out 17 batters, and collected a 1-0 run victory when he scored himself.

Necciai fanned 20 batters in his next start and Bell, not to be one-upped, went out on May 26 and pitched his second consecutive no-hitter, beating Bluefield, W. Va., 4-0.

Enough was not enough, though. With Necciai in the majors in Pittsburgh, Bell went out and pitched a third no-hitter for Bristol on August 25, again setting down Bluefield by the same 4-0 score.

What could Bristol then do for an encore?

On August 26, the night after Bell's third no-hitter, Bristol's Ramsey (not to be outshone) blanked Bluefield again, 1-0—in a no-hitter!

Fastest Pitches Ever Recorded

When a pitcher strikes out 19, 9 and 19 big leaguers in three consecutive games, it's quite clear that he has something on the ball. For Nolan Ryan, the record-breaking right-hander of the California Angels, it was speed. Legitimate 100 mile-an-hour speed. In fact, when Ryan's fastball was timed during the final game of that marvelous stretch in 1974, two of his pitches were clocked at 100.9 mph each—the fastest throws ever recorded. They broke the long-lasting mark of 98.6, set by Bob (Rapid Robert) Feller in 1946.

In fairness to old-time pitchers such as Walter Johnson, the post-World War II mound whizzes have had the benefit of electronic timing devices. There just wasn't any way of clocking the speedball kings before Feller had U.S. Army equipment time his warmup pitches at Griffith Stadium, Washington, D.C., in August, 1946.

But Ryan's dazzling record with more than 4,000 strikeouts in his career—including a record 383 in 1973—supports his claim to the speed king title. No one else has ever topped 100 under electronic surveillance, and he did it more than once and during game conditions.

Ryan's two 100.9-mph pitches were posted exactly 28 years to the day after Feller turned in his 98.6. Ryan first did it when he faced Detroit Tiger leadoff man Ron LeFlore in the first inning of an August 20, 1974, game. He matched that speed later in the game en route to a 19-strikeout, 11-inning game—which he lost, 1-0.

Two and a half weeks later, Ryan was timed again and nearly equaled his record by throwing the ball 100.8 mph. And that was in the ninth inning as he pitched a tough, tight game against the Chicago White Sox. Actually, Ryan had been tested in five pregame warmup pitches but could do no better than 88.5 mph.

The Ryan tests were done with sophisticated equipment provided by a group of Rockwell International scientists. They used an infrared radar device which was placed in the Angel press box.

The record didn't set too well with Ryan, though. He expressed indifference to being clocked—the Angels had made a major publicity drive for the White Sox game—under game conditions.

"I don't like to do it because it takes too much away from my concentration," said Ryan after the game. "Any time you do something like that you've got to be prepared for the worst and I'm glad to get it over."

Among the ten fastest pitchers with official clockings over 90 miles an hour are five (Don Drysdale, Steve Barber, Herb Score, Ryne Duren, and Sandy Koufax) who made it on the same day. In 1960, they and Bob Turley took part in a test arranged by a national magazine during spring training. All were clocked over 90 mph. Turley, who finished last in the test, had joined the "90-mph Club" in 1958, when he was timed at 94.2.

But perhaps the most interesting member of the 90-mph group is Steve Dalkowski, a one-time farmhand of the Baltimore Orioles. He was taken out to Aberdeen Proving Grounds, the military post near Baltimore, and was clocked at 93.5 in 1958. He may have been even faster but he wasn't pitching from a mound (as Feller and others had done), and the wild-throwing speedballer had to throw for 40 minutes in warmups just trying to find the range of the testing equipment. There are those who claim Dalkowski may have been the fastest ever. But his lack of control kept him out of the major leagues.

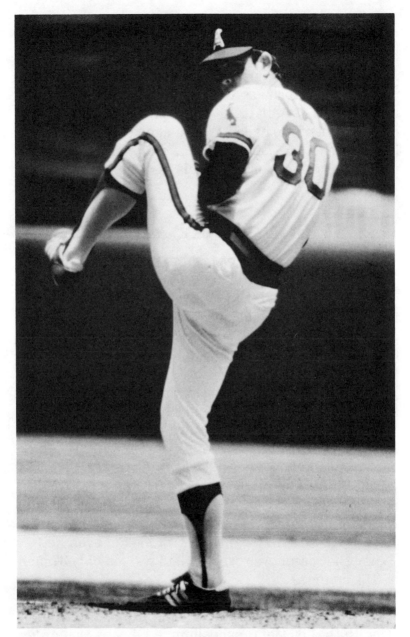

Nolan Ryan has been baseball's greatest "whiz kid."

His strikeout records as a professional are awesome: 1,396 in 995 innings during nine years in the minor leagues. But then again, his walks were awesome, too: 1,345. As a high-school pitcher he once walked 8 men in a no-hit performance. As a pro, he both struck out and walked 21 batters in separate outings. He dropped out of pro ball in 1966 at age 26. His 46-80 won-lost record and 5.67 earned run average just weren't the right stuff to go along with his fastball.

Strikes Out Six All-Stars in Two Innings

The crowd of 50,000 at big-league baseball's second annual All-Star Game in 1934 was in for an early disappointment. The game was being played at the Polo Grounds in New York City and the host team's favorite hero, pitcher Carl Hubbell of the New York Giants, was in deep trouble. Charlie Gehringer of the Detroit Tigers had led off with a single and Heinie Manush of the Washington Senators had drawn a walk. Hubbell had not gotten anyone out in the first inning.

The walk is what rattled the fans. Hubbell just wasn't the type of pitcher to give free passes to opposing batsmen. In fact, the year before, Hubbell had walked only 47 men in 309 innings. In 1934, up to the July 10 All-Star Game, his control looked even better. (When the season was over, he had walked only 37 men in 313 innings.)

Worse yet, the National League's Hubbell had to face the American Leaguers' fearsome Murderer's Row— Babe Ruth, Lou Gehrig and Jimmie Foxx, in that order.

Carl Hubbell was an All-Star who could baffle other All-Stars.

Though he was pitching before his own fans, Hubbell felt some hostility in the crowd.

"I could hear the guys in the stands yelling, 'Take him out before it's too late,' " Hubbell said.

IIis own National League teammates gathered

around him after the walk to Manush. They wanted to be reassured.

"I'm all right," Hubbell told them.

Sure enough, the gangly left-hander was.

Babe Ruth was in the twilight of his career in 1934, but he still was a menacing slugger coming off a season in which he hit 34 homers and batted over .300. He still was a terror with men on base.

But Hubbell reared back, kicking his right foot high in the air, and let loose with his "patented" screwball. Hubbell threw three of them past Ruth, who looked as bewildered as he had ever been in his life. Three times the ball whizzed past the Babe, and three times the game's most famous slugger watched them go past without swinging. Ruth looked at the umpire as the third strike passed by him. He took the bat off his shoulder and headed back to the dugout. "He wasn't mad," Hubbell recalled later. "He just didn't believe it."

Hubbell may have been back in the groove, but he had to face Gehrig next—and, unlike Ruth, Lou was at the peak of his career. He was in the midst of a season in which he would win the triple crown—leading the league in batting, homeruns, and RBI's.

Hubbell cooly kept hurling screwballs. Gehrig was almost as befuddled as Ruth had been, and that was rare, for Gehrig was at his best with men on base. Hubbell needed four pitches to set down Gehrig for his second straight strikeout.

Foxx was as fearsome as Gehrig. He had won the triple crown the year before with 48 homers, 163 RBI's and a .356 batting average. The star of the Philadelphia A's stared at his National League opponent as the two base runners got ready to move.

As Hubbell tossed a strike past Foxx, the base runners Gehringer and Manush worked a double steal. That meant that just one of Foxx's long singles would bring them home. Hubbell braced himself and threw another strike past Foxx. Then, without a trace of fear, Hubbell got him on the third pitch.

King Carl had thrown ten pitches to three of the greatest sluggers ever—and struck out all three of them. He had defied all baseball odds.

But Hubbell wasn't through.

In the second inning, the American League's leadoff man was Al Simmons, a steady .300 hitter. The Chicago White Sox outfielder had reached .300 ten years in a row and was about to do it again in 1934. In 1930 and 1931 he had batted .381 and .390 to lead his league. Unawed, Hubbell struck him out, too. The he struck out Joe Cronin, the Washington Senator shortstop who had batted over .300 for four straight years.

Never had one pitcher set down five dangerous future Hall of Famers in such fashion.

The spell couldn't last forever. Bill Dickey, the New York Yankees' ace catcher, singled to break the streak. But Hubbell came back strong to fan the pitcher, Lefty Gomez, for his sixth strikeout in two innings of All-Star play. He pitched one more inning of scoreless ball, then left the game with the National League in command, 4-0.

Without him, the National League All-Stars fell apart and finally lost, 9-7. But few were concerned with the score when the Polo Grounds emptied. Most of them agreed with league president Joe Heydler, who said it was the greatest feat he had seen in 60 years of watching baseball.

Fernando Valenzuela, the Los Angeles Dodger pitcher, finally matched Hubbell's feat in the 1986 All-Star game. But his six victims included a pitcher.

Longest Career in Pitching

In his first time at bat as a major leaguer, Hoyt Wilhelm hit a homerun. Only 51 others have ever done that in their first time up in the majors, and what's more, Wilhelm never hit another homer even though he played in 1,070 major-league games.

However, Hoyt Wilhelm stopped more than his share of potential homerun hitters in his record 21 years as a pitcher. He won a record total of 123 games as a reliever and saved a record 227 more games. Though relief pitching is a precarious way of making a living, Wilhelm went from the bullpen to starting pitcher, which may have been the most amazing feat of all for the rubbery-armed right-hander.

Wilhelm was the kind of steady player that teams loved to pick up in the heat of a pennant race. He was good almost to the end that way. In 1971, the year before he retired, he was released by the Atlanta Braves and seemingly was through at age 48. But he signed with the Spokane, Wash., team in the minor leagues after he obtained his unconditional release from Atlanta—and made it back to the majors in September when Spokane's parent team, the Los Angeles Dodgers, needed a reliable arm in their quest for a National League pennant.

Wilhelm pitched in nine games for the Dodgers and gave up only two earned runs in 18 innings. His famed knuckleball could still baffle wide-eyed hitters half his age.

Anybody who knows baseball knows that the knuckleball takes less out of a pitcher physically than any other pitch short of a lob. Wilhelm was the first person to credit the pitch with prolonging his career.

"I don't say it doesn't take anything out of you at

Nobody ever provided more relief than Hoyt Wilhelm. In 21 years he pitched in a record 1,070 games.

all," he said in his final season in the majors, "but I've never had to rear back and try to throw the ball by the hitters."

But 21 years is long by any standards. As the late baseball expert Milton Richman wrote about the amazing Wilhelm's career, "Even those mechanical pitching machines break down before 30 years."

Strangely enough, Hoyt Wilhelm spent a decade pitching in the minors before he ever got to the big time. He signed as a 19-year-old in 1942. When he finally got to the majors, with the New York Giants in 1952, he was an immediate sensation. The Giants pitched him in relief for a near-record 71 games and Wilhelm responded by winning 15, losing only three and leading the National League with an earned run average of 2.43 that year. He was the league's Rookie of the Year.

Wilhelm continued to make about 50 relief appearances a year for the next 6 years until 1958, when the Cleveland Indians decided to give him a few starts. The rival Baltimore Orioles liked what they saw in the 35-year-old starter and got him from Cleveland.

Throughout 1959, Wilhelm was a full-time starter—and a good one. Hoyt started 27 games and completed 13 of them for the Orioles in 1959. He pitched three shutouts and led the American League with a 2.19 earned run average. His 15-11 record was quite impressive considering the weak hitting team he played for.

But relief pitchers were becoming almost as valuable as starters by the end of the 1950s, so Baltimore moved him into the bullpen where he again began making about 50 appearances per year. He was traded to the Chicago White Sox in 1963. They used him mostly in relief, too, though he did start three games for them. After '63, Hoyt was strictly a bullpen man, making the 300-foot hike to the mound game after game in clutch situations.

In 1964, he won 12 games and saved 27 others for one of his finest seasons. For five straight years, he held his ERA below 2.00.

The years kept being added to his pitching record.

"At first, I felt I could hang on for five years," he said. "When I made five, I felt I could last ten. After that, I saw no reason why I couldn't go 15, then 20. And here I am."

At one point, he found himself pitching his knuckler in spring training to a befuddled young catcher who was born *after* Hoyt reached the majors.

The late Paul Richards, the clever baseball manager who had Wilhelm in Baltimore, picked him up again in Atlanta and suggested in 1970 that Hoyt could probably pitch "another hundred years."

But time eventually caught up with him in 1972, when he made his last big-league appearance with the Los Angeles Dodgers. As he attended his final spring training sessions, he was asked what was the biggest change he had seen in baseball during more than two decades.

Wilhelm's answer was fitting: "I'd have to say it's got to do with the relief pitcher. He's become more predominant."

Relief Is Just a Second Away

Anyone who has heard those television commercials about how you can get relief in minutes can appreciate the feats of some relief pitchers who provided relief in seconds. For instance, Jim Davis, a Chicago Cubs' pitcher, was trying to slow down the St. Louis Cardinals in 1956 as the game moved into the sixth inning. The southpaw was doing a good job. He struck out Hal Smith, Jim Brandt and Lindy McDaniel. But the third strike to McDaniel got away from the catcher, allowing a man on third to score and McDaniel to get to first base safely. Davis wasn't rattled by his ill fate, however. He calmly struck out Don Blasingame—Davis' fourth "K" of the inning—to become the first pitcher since 1916 to fan four batters in an inning.

*   *   *

In relief jobs, though, the minors have outshone the majors. Take Tony Komisar, a former left-hander for the Leesburg Braves in the Florida State League. He came into the nightcap of a 1956 game with Daytona Beach and faced a tough ninth-inning assignment. His team was ahead, 6-3, but Daytona Beach had the bases loaded. On his first pitch, the batter lined to the third baseman, who quickly tagged the base for the second out and relayed the ball to second for a triple play. One pitch, three outs. For Komisar, it was sweet revenge. Earlier in the day, he had lost a 12-inning pitching duel to the same Daytona Beach team.

Bill Harrington, pitching relief for Charleston, W. Va., of the American Association, matched Komisar's three-kills-on-one pitch a year later in a game against

Louisville. Harrington got a little relief himself out of the accomplishment, because he was protecting a three-run lead with the bases loaded when a Louisville slugger hit what seemed to be a sure homerun smash to centerfield. As the baserunners began to head for home, Harrington's centerfielder made a miraculous catch and threw the ball for the second out into second base, where it was sent on to third for the triple play.

In a third case, Bruce Haroldson got three out on one pitch when he was hurling for Lewistown, Idaho, in the 1950s.

*   *   *

Steve Kraly of the Nashville team in the Southern Association didn't get three outs on one pitch, but he once collected two victories while facing just two men. It happened in 1959 when the left-hander was pitching relief. On June 9, he came into a game against Mobile with his team behind in the ninth inning. There were two outs. Kraly struck out the only man he faced, then sat back and watched Nashville rally for three runs in the bottom of the inning to win for him, 4-3.

Three days later, Kraly made his next appearance. This time he came in with two outs in the eighth and his team again on the short end of the score. Kraly got the opposing Atlanta player to ground out. Then he was lifted for a pinch hitter, who conveniently helped Nashville rally and take a 3-2 victory. Kraly had won two games and pitched to only two batters.

• II •
Zeroing In on History

The Most Perfect Innings

In the visitors' clubhouse of Milwaukee's County Stadium, on May 26, 1959, pitcher Harvey Haddix ran down the Milwaukee Braves' lineup for the benefit of his teammates and methodically told how he planned to pitch to each opponent. It was routine stuff for the Pittsburgh Pirates' left-handed hurler and his teammates. But this night, one of the Pirate players offered a comment to encourage Haddix, who had not been getting much onfield support.

"That was a good rundown, Harvey," said third baseman Don Hoak. "You go out there and pitch to those guys exactly like that and you'll pitch a no-hitter."

As it turned out, Haddix did more than that.

The first man to face Haddix that evening was the Braves' Johnny O'Brien. Haddix tested his fastball on O'Brien and came up with a strike. Next, he tried his slider and that too was on target. He made a quick decision to rely on those pitches for the rest of the night.

Haddix, a 33-year-old hurler with a sketchy big-league career, got O'Brien and the rest of the side out in the first, and again in the second. Pirate shortstop Dick Schofield made a leaping snare of a line drive that looked headed for a safety in the third. Again in the sixth, Schofield made a long throw out of a deep ground ball that would certainly have gone through for a single. Otherwise, Haddix was getting out every Brave who faced him—in the order they faced him.

It occurred to Haddix that he had a no-hitter going because the crowd, even though it was pro-Milwaukee, was rallying behind him. But it didn't dawn on Haddix that he was pitching a perfect no-hit game.

Besides, Haddix had other problems to worry about. He personally was off to a good start that season, but his teammates just weren't giving him much scoring support. The Pirates were repeating their lackluster offense this night, too, even though they were getting more than their share of hits off the Braves' Lew Burdette.

In fact, the Pirates were to get 12 hits for the game. But all of them were singles. In the third inning alone, the Pirates got three hits and failed to score; one of the singles hitters had been thrown out when he tried to stretch an extra base out of a teammate's single.

With two outs in the ninth, Haddix had a perfect game at the brink—something only four other pitchers had done in the majors in the 20th Century. When Burdette, the 27th batter, came up to the plate, he shouted out something about breaking up the no-hitter. Haddix may have been rattled somewhat by the opposing pitcher's comment, because he brought the count to 2-2. Then his catcher, Smokey Burgess, called for a slider to polish off Burdette. Haddix sent a good one that Burdette swung at and missed. It was his eighth strikeout.

Haddix had his perfect nine innings—but no victory yet.

Still, the Milwaukee crowd of 19,000 stood up and gave him a rousing cheer.

The Pirates came to bat in the top of the tenth, eager to help their masterful pitcher claim his piece of history. With one out and a man on first base, hefty Dick Stuart, the team's homerun hitter, smacked a ball that carried all the way to the centerfield fence. But the Braves' Andy Pafko chased it down, caught it, and prevented the run.

Since the scoreboard at County Stadium registered only ten innings, Haddix lost track of just how well he was doing. He became confused as to what inning it was.

But he continued to check the Braves in perfect fashion, getting them out in order in the tenth, eleventh and twelfth innings, too. No pitcher before or since has ever pitched more than the full nine innings of perfect ball. Haddix had had 36 men come up and gone back frustrated.

The 165-pounder watched as his team went stale in the thirteenth inning, too. He also saw them tensing up a bit in the field. In the bottom of the thirteenth inning, Haddix' string of perfection came to an end. Don Hoak's throwing error after a grounder by Felix Mantilla let the Braves' leadoff man get on first. The Pirates made a feeble protest that Mantilla had made a wrong turn at first, but the complaint was not allowed.

Mantilla was sacrificed to second base, so strategy dictated that Haddix should intentionally walk the next batter, Hank Aaron, which he did. It was the only walk Haddix gave up all night.

Joe Adcock, the Braves' husky first baseman, was the next man up. He had struck out twice and grounded out two other times to become a routine victim for Haddix. But in the thirteenth, Haddix slipped a pitch at him that was just too high. Haddix realized that fact when he let the ball go. By then, it was too late. Adcock got under the pitch and lifted it toward left-center. The Pirates' Bill Virdon, who had made two fine deep catches in the tenth inning, raced furiously and leaped for the ball—but it was slightly over the fence and out of reach. Mantilla jaunted toward home to score.

Yet in a strange wrapup to a strange game, Aaron left the playing field after touching second base. Braves players and fans yelled for him to continue circling the bases but Aaron didn't hear them until it was too late; Adcock had already passed him on the bases. Due to the technicality, which wasn't resolved till the next day, Haddix lost 1-0, instead of 3-0. It was hardly much consolation for the man who had pitched the most consecutive perfect innings in baseball history.

Losing Pitcher, Big Winner

The Detroit Tigers had gone 52 years without ever finishing in last place in their league—an amazing stretch that no other team could claim in 1952. But that year their luck ran out and they floundered miserably from start to finish, 45 games behind the league-leading New York Yankees. Good players turned sour overnight. Those who played well got little support from their teammates, so their talents were unnoticed.

One such victim was Virgil (Fire) Trucks, the 33-year-old fastball pitcher who once set an organized baseball record for strikeouts with 418 for a minor-league team. Trucks, when going right, was a potential 20-game winner. He had reached 19 one season and in ten major-league campaigns had never had a losing season.

But in 1952, the roof caved in on him, too.

That year, Trucks pitched in 35 games. He started 29. He won only five, compared with 19 losses.

That season, though, Trucks' five victories included two no-hitters, a one-hitter, a two-hitter and a six-hitter. Considering that the Tigers had not had a pitcher give a no-hit performance in some 40 years, Trucks' achievements are all the more amazing.

Trucks' first no-hitter in the majors (he had had four in the minors) came against the Washington Senators on May 15, 1952. The burly pitcher didn't pitch that impressively, however, as no-hitters go. He hit two batters, walked another and saw one man get on by error. It took a ninth-inning home run by Vic Wertz to give him a 1-0 victory.

Victories came few and far between after that. In another encounter with the Senators, Trucks no-hit them after giving up a single in the first inning. By the time the Tigers departed for an Eastern swing in August, Trucks was on the trading block, and players were coming and going by the numbers in Detroit. The team was playing so poorly that not one sportswriter among Detroit's three major daily newspapers bothered to accompany the team to New York for an August 25th game with the Yankees. Trucks, with a mere 4-15 record, was about to take on the best team in baseball.

Trucks' control was remarkably better than it had been for most of the year, including the first no-hitter, as he began leveling the Yankees. He was loose and mixing his pitches and relying on control more than on his vaunted fastball.

He set down the Yankees in the first and second innings, then ran into a small problem in the third. It was then that Phil Rizzuto slapped a grounder at Tiger shortstop Johnny Pesky, who seemed to have trouble getting

Virgil Trucks had 19 losses and only 5 victories in 1952. But, oh, what victories those 5 were.

the ball out of his glove. When Pesky did free up the ball, he made a late and low throw to first base. Rizzuto got on.

The official scorer first gave Pesky an error. Then, after checking with press box colleagues, he changed it to a hit. The scoreboard listed a hit and that's the way it stayed until the seventh inning. Then, during the stretch, an announcement was made that the decision had been reversed back to an error after further consultation.

The crowd of 13,442 Yankee fans suddenly came alive. Some of them may have seen Allie Reynolds pitch two no-hitters the year before, but that was for a championship team. The Tigers were nobodies.

As the game wore on, Trucks got better and better. After allowing three men on in the first inning (one by a walk, two by errors), Trucks bore down and retired batter after batter. In the meantime, Steve Souchak—Wertz' replacement—knocked in a run to give Trucks a 1-0 lead.

The Yankees had never been no-hitted before during a pennant race. But Trucks had their number that day. He continued his dominance until the final inning, then relied on a fastball to get him through his second no-hitter of the year. As it was, he retired the final 22 Yankees in a row. Again he won, 1-0, for his final moment of success in a startlingly unusual year.

The following season Trucks was traded not once but twice. Strangely enough, 1953 turned out to be his first 20-game winning year.

The Only World Series No-Hitter

Perfect was not the best word to use in describing pitcher Don Larsen. "Fun-loving," "carousing," and "Peck's Bad Boy" were used more often. The big 6-foot-4-inch strongman with the face of a movie star had a casual aura about him, even in what hardened baseball people considered the most crucial situations. The *New York Times* once reported that, "On a Yankee squad that includes a liberal share of *bon vivants*, Larsen has had the reputation of being one of the gayest blades."

Larsen seemed to have his own set of training rules. That got him in trouble more than once. As for not making the best of his talents, the Yankees returned him to the minors in 1955, his first year with the club, as sort of a shape-up side trip.

But Larsen had talent to spare. The Yankees got him in the first place—as one of the key figures in an 18-man trade—despite the fact that he was a miserable 3-21 with the Baltimore Orioles in 1954. That first season with the Yankees, Larsen was recalled in late July from his minor-league demotion, and posted an 8-1 record to help the team win the American League pennant. He celebrated the strong finish the next spring by driving his brand new convertible into a telephone pole at 5 A.M. after a late date.

The Yankees kept him throughout 1956, however, because he was resourceful on the pitching mound, at least. He posted an 11-5 record as a part-time starter and long reliever.

"The big feller can be one of the greatest if he wants to be," Casey Stengel, the Yankee manager, used to say often about the 220-pound Larsen. Stengel used to marvel at all Larsen's talents—his ability to hit and field

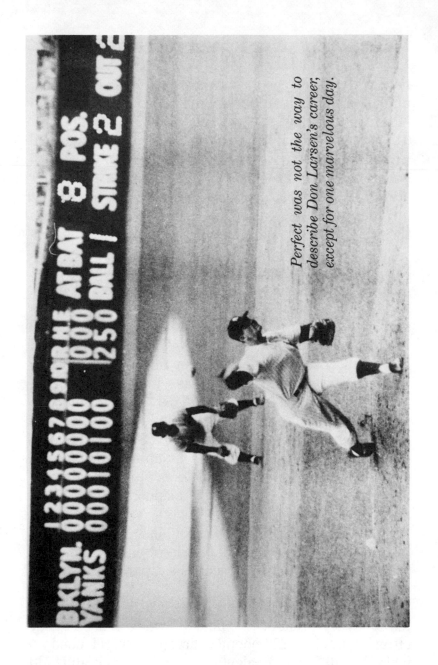

Perfect was not the way to describe Don Larsen's career, except for one marvelous day.

and run the bases as well as pitch. Larsen was sometimes used as a pinch hitter and pinch runner, too.

But in general the "big feller" didn't have a distinguished major-league career. He stuck around for 14 years but won only 81 games and lost 91.

For one day, though, Larsen was as perfect as any pitcher can be. It happened on October 8, 1956, at the end of his second year with the Yankees.

There was nothing unusual about the day except for the fact that Stengel decided to take a chance with Larsen in the fifth World Series game against the powerful Brooklyn Dodgers. It was chancy for several reasons, the main one being Larsen's sometimes erratic moves. Stengel remembered that Larsen had been rattled in the second game of the 1956 Series, when he went into the second inning with a 6-0 lead and began to blow it. He had yanked Larsen then, before the Dodgers went on to win the game, 13-8. But now Casey was having trouble with his pitchers; so he went to Larsen in the fifth game, with the Series tied, three days after the 13-8 debacle.

Larsen had one strong point: He didn't let games affect him beforehand. The 27-year-old righthander prepped for his third World Series start by having a few beers and turning in past midnight. "I just did like I always do," he said nonchalantly.

But the next day, before a packed crowd of 64,000 at Yankee Stadium, he did more than usual.

Larsen got hooked up in a pitching duel with the Dodgers' tough Sal Maglie. Larsen set down the first 12 Dodgers to face him. Not one of them got to base. Maglie meanwhile mowed down the first 11 Yankees he encountered.

A home run by the Yankees' Mickey Mantle broke

the ice in the bottom of the fourth. But Larsen's spell over the Dodgers continued.

Larsen was getting some help. Yogi Berra behind the plate was handling Larsen beautifully, mixing up his array of fastballs, sliders and slow curves. Afield, the Yanks were contributing their usual collection of outstanding plays, too. Shortstop Gil McDougald snatched a hard-hit ball by Jackie Robinson off the ground after it had caromed from third baseman Andy Carey's glove and McDougald made the throw to first to get Robinson. Mantle made a brilliant dash to get a long-hit ball by Gil Hodges in the fifth inning.

But the triumph was mostly Larsen's as he handled a lineup including a half dozen Hall of Fame prospects with relative ease. Only once did Larsen give as many as three balls to one batter. Seven times he struck out Dodger batters. Only four batted balls could even be considered potential hits under the right conditions, and one of those four was a foul.

The Yankees got an insurance run when Hank Bauer homered. Then they nervously watched Larsen try to pitch the first perfect game since 1922. The idea of accomplishing the feat in the World Series added to the tension. In fact, no pitcher had ever hurled a no-hitter in World Series play.

Larsen continued to dazzle the likes of Roy Campanella, Pee Wee Reese, Duke Snider, Carl Furillo, Robinson and Hodges with his no-windup delivery. And with the game less than two hours old, it came down to Larsen versus pinch hitter Dale Mitchell, an ex-American Leaguer with a .312 lifetime batting average.

Mitchell was batting for Maglie. There were two outs in the ninth and Larsen had retired 26 men in a row.

Larsen first threw a ball. The stadium was so quiet

you could almost hear the sweat roll down the players' faces. Larsen got back on target; he next threw to a corner and came up with a called strike. Mitchell swung at the next pitch and missed. Then he fouled off a ball. Mitchell had been taking his time, which rattled Larsen a little bit. But the pitcher countered this strategy by throwing fast—and hard.

His next pitch was a fastball that zoomed over the plate. Umpire Babe Pinelli promptly called it strike three—the clincher to what may have been baseball's best-pitched game considering the circumstances and the competition.

High-School Kid with 0.18 ERA

The Texas Rangers had heard so much about a high-school phenom in 1973 that they decided to send their key front-office personnel out to watch 18-year-old David Clyde pitch. Rangers owner Bob Short, general manager Joe Burke, manager Whitey Herzog and pitching coach Chuck Estrada all ventured out to a high-school field in Dallas when Clyde came to town with his Houston Westchester High team.

Clyde didn't disappoint them. He went about his business of pitching his ninth no-hitter of the year against Dallas' Kimball High, striking out two batters every inning and getting a 1-0 victory.

If Clyde wasn't the most sensational high-school pitcher ever, he had to be close. He completed his senior year with an 18-0 record. His earned run average was a next-to-nothing 0.18. Clyde struck out 328 batters in 148 innings.

His no-hitter in front of the Rangers' management paid off handsomely for the left-hander, too. When the baseball draft of free agents was held that year, the Rangers made him the first player to be taken. They paid him a $125,000 bonus to assure that they would get him, too.

Nineteen days after he graduated from high school, he was on the mound for the Rangers, pitching a 4-3 victory.

In no time at all, the Rangers got that bonus money back. Clyde drew over 113,000 fans for his first four starts.

Fortunately for the Rangers, the repayment came soon. Clyde's fortunes—on the field, at least—fizzled and he was out of the majors right after his 24th birthday.

• III •
Long-Ball Sluggers

Tape-Measure Homers

Mickey Mantle was a country boy who could hit the ball a country mile. Mantle was a mere 21 years old when crusty New York Yankee Manager Casey Stengel made the comment, "He is probably the most powerful switch hitter the game has ever known." Stengel was perhaps a little partial to his own player, but his baseball wisdom had been accumulated over four decades. Besides, the year he made the comment—1953—Casey had some other figures to back him up.

Mantle was a third-year major leaguer at the time and just coming into his own as a homerun hitter. He had hit 37 doubles in 1952, but at 21 he was better muscled and getting his full 175 pounds into the swing.

In 1953 his homeruns weren't just dropping over fences—they were going well beyond them. It was Mantle who created a new, though unofficial, statistic called the "tape-measure homer." He turned sportswriters and public relations men into surveyors when he awed them with his long-distance booms.

Mantle gave a preview of things to come for the 1953 season in an exhibition game at Pittsburgh's Forbes Field on the eve of the regular season. Batting left-handed, he poled a ball over the rightfield seats and out of the ballpark, a feat only two men (one was Babe Ruth) had ever done.

Then eight days later, on April 17, with the regular season under way, Mantle struck again.

Left-hander Chuck Stobbs was one of the better pitchers on the old Washington Senators' team; so Mantle naturally batted right-handed against him.

Mantle got hold of one of Stobbs' pitches and launched it toward the bleachers in left-center. The ball picked up momentum plus a bit of a tailwind as it sailed over the heads of the fans at Griffith Stadium. It passed the 460-foot mark, where they sat, then bounced off a 60-foot-high sign. It came to a rest in a backyard. The figure filberts were so intrigued they measured the distance. It turned out to be 565 feet from home plate.

Other balls, perhaps off the bat of Babe Ruth, may have gone further. Ruth supposedly blasted one 587 feet in an exhibition game in St. Petersburg, Fla. But Mantle's blow was measured and to this day is the standard.

Mantle grew to be 195 pounds and was a more powerful hitter, when in 1956 he came close to poking a ball out of Yankee Stadium; it hit the façade at the top of the third deck in rightfield.

In 1963, he tagged a ball pitched by the Kansas City Athletics' reliever Bill Fischer and sent it to nearly the same place. It was still rising when it crashed off a 108-foot-high façade atop the third deck. Statisticians estimated the ball would have traveled perhaps 620 feet without the obstruction. A year later, he got his power behind a pitch by Ray Herbert of the Chicago White Sox and sent it over 500 feet into dead centerfield at Yankee Stadium for the longest measured homer at his home park.

Mantle's longest homer had to be figured out using trigonometry. A baseball historian figured in 1985, after an exhaustive study of facts he dug up, that a Mantle homer on September 10, 1960, had traveled 643 feet in all, after first sailing over the rightfield roof of Tiger Stadium in Detroit and landing in a lumberyard.

"730-Foot" Homer

Gil Carter was an all-around athlete and a "slugger" in every sport he took up. As a 210-pound heavyweight boxer, he won 61 of 68 bouts. As a football player, he made all-state in Kansas for his hard-hitting plunges from fullback. But it was in baseball that he really made a name for himself with his hard hitting.

Playing for Carlsbad, N.M., of the Sophomore League in 1959, the 23-year-old outfielder was zooming in on that minor league's homerun record. He finally got the record with his 28th of the season on August 11—and left a few people gaping in disbelief in the process.

Homer No. 28 for Carter took off like a shot toward the leftfield fence. It was still rising when it soared over a light tower 360 feet from home plate. The ball kept on going, crossing a street, two alleys and two lots. Then it disappeared from sight. Later, a developer of a subdivision behind the ballpark found the ball beside a house, 730 feet from home plate. En route to the house it knocked some peaches from a tree.

The people who took the time to analyze the homer said it had to travel at least 650 feet before the bounces and rolls that carried it to the 730-foot mark. Nobody has *officially* recorded the longest homerun in history, but the hard-hitting Carter has to be right up there with the distance sluggers.

70-Foot "Homer"

What may have been the shortest homerun on record in major-league baseball occurred one hot summer day in 1914 at Washington Park in Brooklyn. It happened in a Federal League game between the Brooklyn Feds and the Chicago Whales. The league was considered an "outlaw circuit," but nevertheless it was made up of very good teams and players, and has been accorded major-league status by most baseball historians.

Only two umpires handled a game in those days—one behind the plate and another in the infield. But one of the umpires failed to show for a regularly scheduled game at Washington Park on a very hot summer day. The other ump, Bill Brennan, decided to work alone.

Brennan got tired of racing to the home dugout each time he ran out of new balls, so before the fifth inning he built a pyramid of them behind the pitcher's mound, from where he was calling balls and strikes.

In the fifth, Brooklyn catcher Grover Land, who had only three homers to show for his five years with the Cleveland Indians in the American League, smacked a line drive into the pile of balls about 70 feet away and splattered them in all directions. Land took off running for first, realizing that he had created a rare confusion.

The Chicago infielders couldn't sort through the balls to find out which was the right one, so they conveniently picked up any ball near them and tagged away at Land as he circled the bases. Land just keep on running. When he reached home plate, the Chicago catcher was waiting for him with one of the balls, too—but the overworked umpire disregarded that tag also.

Land was given credit for an "inside the park" homer.

72 Homeruns One Season

Babe Ruth's major-league homerun record of 60 in one season seemed out of sight during the early years of the 1950's. But for a gigantic minor leaguer who would never make the majors, the Ruthian-size records were not so significant. In four years, from 1952 through 1955, Joltin' Joe Bauman slugged 221 home runs—an average of more than 58 a season.

Bauman, a strapping 6-foot-5-inch, 240-pound first baseman, had been counted out of the major-league picture by scouts when he began his spree in 1952. He was already 30 years old, and he pretty much muffed his big-league hopes when he clubbed only 11 homeruns and batted .275 for the Hartford, Conn., team of the Class A Eastern League back in 1948. That's as high as Bauman ever got as a Boston Brave farmhand. The fact that the Braves were a pennant winner in 1948 left them with little time to groom Bauman for the majors even though he had smashed 48 and 38 homers in two previous seasons. Bauman himself studied the situation and figured it hopeless, dropping out of organized ball to play for a semi-pro team in Oklahoma after the 1948 season.

But pro ball lured Bauman back in 1952. He got reinstated and joined the Artesia, N. M. team of the Class C Longhorn League.

It took little time for Joe Bauman to get back in the groove. He smacked an even 50 homers that season and had the league's pitchers so shaken up that on one occasion a right-handed hurler actually pitched left-handed to the left-handed-hitting Bauman in an effort to stymie him. (The strategy worked, by the way. In one of the few—if not the only—cases of ambidextrous pitching on record, Audie Malone of the Roswell team carried Bauman to a 3-2 count and then struck him out with a slow curve!)

Bauman kept tearing up the league and became a local hero. He hit 53 more homeruns for Artesia in 1953, then joined the Roswell team in another New Mexico city. Come 1954 and the slugging first baseman, who had been playing minor-league baseball since 1941, began making history. He had his eye set on the all-time organized baseball record of 69 homers, established by Joe Hauser of the Minneapolis team of the American Association back in 1933, and tied by Bob Crues of the Amarillo, Texas, team in 1948.

Bauman zeroed in on that mark on August 31 when he smashed four homers against Sweetwater to bring his total up to 68. That left Bauman four games in which to match or surpass Hauser, an ex-Philadelphia Athletic who had made his mark after a six-year major-league stay, and Crues.

In his next game, Bauman just missed the fence by inches as he lined a long-shot foul. Then on September 2, he caught Hauser with his 69th.

Bauman had accomplished his first 69 in only 136 games, which was remarkable in its own right. Hauser, for example, needed 154 games for his feat and Crues 140.

Now Bauman had two more games—a September 5 doubleheader at his old stomping grounds in Artesia—in which he could claim the record for himself. The twin-bill evoked enough interest to draw an overflow 2,600 fans to NuMex Park.

Bauman tried not to let them down. In the first inning, after taking a 2-2 count from the pitcher, Bauman fouled off two more pitches. Then boom! The Roswell

Rocket lofted the ball 360 feet and over the fence for home run No. 70. He could now relax.

Bauman's idea of relaxing was to smack homeruns. He got two more in the second game to bring his season total to 72.

Naturally Bauman had his share of critics—the people who scoffed at the Class C level of play, the depleted minor-league ranks because of the Korean War, and the short fences that minor leaguers enjoy. But an overall look at Bauman's 1954 season lends luster to his accomplishments.

In addition to his 72 homeruns in 498 official at-bats, Joe batted an even .400 and drove in 224 runs for a second-place team. He struck out 99 times while he was swinging for the big ones, but he also was hampered in his quest by 150 walks.

As for the short fences, well. . . .

After the windup of the regular season, Roswell entered the Longhorn League playoffs. In one game, against Carlsbad, Joe Bauman tagged a ball and sent it flying approximately 500 feet. Few big leaguers have hit one that far.

Long Balls and a Short Fence

The Corsicana team of the Texas League was loaded with good hitters in 1902, so many in fact that a promising young Canadian-born prospect named Justin (Nig) Clarke was placed seventh in the batting order. Clarke, a 19-year-old catcher destined for the major leagues, could not complain, however. Corsicana was so good that it busted the Texas League pennant race wide open by winning 27 straight games. It was one of the best minor-league clubs ever assembled.

But after a June 15 game with Texarkana, the "Oil City" team may have wondered if they had underestimated the teenage backstop. That day he had eight official at-bats and eight shots at the short (estimated at 200 to 220 feet) fence of the ballpark at Ennis, Texas. He made the best of them—by slugging eight homeruns.

All in all, Clarke had 32 total bases and batted in 16 runs. The box score for the day shows him with a stolen base, which indicates he may have gotten on base by a walk, too.

Clarke carried the brunt of the attack that Sunday afternoon. But he wasn't the only hero for Corsicana. The box score shows the Oil City's Bill Alexander, the shortstop, and Ike Pendleton, the leftfielder and cleanup man, with 8-for-8 at the plate, too. Alexander and first baseman Mike O'Connor each smacked three homers, and the rest of the Corsicana team combined for seven more. The 21 homeruns were instrumental in Corsicana's 51-3 victory.

For years, Clarke's feat came under close scrutiny because one box score of the day had him listed as scoring only three runs. But the team's shortstop and also the club owner made sworn affidavits that Clarke indeed smacked eight homers.

Perhaps the skepticism arose over the fact that Clarke, as a nine-year veteran in the majors, had a grand total of six big-league homeruns.

But for the day in 1902, he was supreme.

Finding the Fences

Back in the days before big-league baseball franchises became a floating crap game, bouncing from city to city as the season comes to an end, the great Babe Ruth set an impressive standard by hitting a homer in every American League ballpark for 11 straight years. Baseball was simple then; a league consisted of eight teams and they stayed put year after year.

A couple of other players set marathon marks, too, by hitting homers in all 15 possible parks—American and National Leagues. They were Harry Heilmann and Johnny Mize. The latter reached his fifteenth different fence (two St. Louis teams shared the same park in those days) when he was 39 years old in 1952. In fact, Mize got the fifteenth ballpark into his portfolio by hitting a grand slammer in Washington.

Nowadays the old parks are replaced by new edifices and teams are shifted from television market area to television market area at the drop of a rating. When the lords of baseball run out of places to shift teams to, they expand the leagues. Baseball has gone from 16 teams in the era of Ruth, Heilmann and Mize to 26—and they may not be done expanding yet.

The new alignments have made it simple to hit in more parks than 15, as Heilmann and Mize had done.

But one of the premier sluggers of recent times is making it difficult for contemporaries to match him for "notches" on his bat. Frank Robinson made Baseball's Hall of Fame for many reasons, including his fourth-place listing on the all-time homerun hitting list (with 586) and his unique honor of being named Most Valuable Player in both the National and American Leagues.

His resourcefulness for knocking down fences

wherever he played stands out most of all. In his career, 1956-76, Robinson has homered in 32 different ballparks during regular-season games.

But Daniel "Rusty" Staub, who played 23 years (1963-85) while the expansion boom was still at its peak, managed to equal Robinson's feat, though he hit only half as many total homeruns in his career.

And perhaps more remarkable was Leo Cardenas, one of Robinson's teammates for a while at Cincinnati, who hit in 26 different parks, even though he had only 118 career homers.

Father and Son Pitch to Ted Williams

Ted Williams' hitting feats smacked of the dramatic. For parts of four different decades, he awed fellow major leaguers with his Herculean hits.

But one family he left a particularly special impression on was Thornton Lee's. Lee was a veteran left-handed pitcher for the Chicago White Sox when Williams came up in 1939. Lee lasted 15 years in the American League and thus got a chance to see more than one Williams' homerun rising over his head while he was on the mound.

Thornton Lee had a son, however.

Don Lee, a right-hander pitching for the Washington Senators, was new to the starting rotation just when Williams was bowing out of baseball in 1960.

On September 2 that year, Williams tagged the younger Lee for a homer, too. It was one of the last few of the 521 he smacked in the big leagues—and perhaps the only time major-league homeruns were hit by the same man against a father and son.

• IV •

Hitting Feats

Five Hits in Five Swings

Stan Musial's batting feats rank alongside Ty Cobb's, Ted Williams' and Pete Rose's.

His career total of 3,630 hits, his seven batting championships, his .376 average in 1948 are testimonials to his greatness. To single out a feat from his 22-year career with the St. Louis Cardinals is a feat in itself.

But in the 1948 season, when he was at his best, Stan The Man came through with an incredible performance to maintain his lofty batting average. Three times that season, Musial had gone 5-for-5 at bat. But on September 22, in a game against the league-leading Boston Braves, Musial was in no shape to repeat his five hits in five at-bats.

He had just been hanging in, suffering from an injured wrist as the season was coming to an end. The batting championship was virtually his, whether he played or not. The next best contender for the title lagged some 40 percentage points behind.

The cold, windy weather that day wasn't in his favor either, but Musial insisted on playing.

On his first time up, he lashed the first pitch for a single.

Next time he came to bat, he doubled on the initial throw.

On his very next time up, he improved his distance hitting by smacking a homerun—his 38th of the season. Again it was on the first pitch.

Musial's left wrist continued to bother him, especially when the left-handed batter tried to pull the ball.

However, it bothered him only physically. Mentally, Musial couldn't have been sharper. The next time he came to bat, he eyed the first pitch thrown him very carefully and singled again. To cap off the day his fifth (and last) time up, he again singled on the first pitch to come his way.

Dozens upon dozens of players had gone 5-for-5, but none had ever gone 5-for-5 on five pitches!

From 0 Hits in 18 At-Bats to 7-for-7

The heavy hitters in baseball never felt threatened when 155-pound Cesar Gutierrez lugged his big 36-ounce bat to the plate during his brief major-league career. There was no way "Cocoa" (as he was nicknamed) was going to dislodge any of their records. The only reason he swung the big bat, he had said himself, was to try to knock a few bloopers over infielders' heads.

Gutierrez didn't make it to the major leagues for his hitting anyway. The Venezuelan was a slick fielding shortstop and utility infielder when he joined the San Francisco Giants in 1967. But his batting was so unimpressive he was shipped to the Detroit Tigers in the American League in 1970. It was there that he finally got a chance—at age 27—to become a regular in the majors.

Stan Musial wasn't best known for his homeruns, but he could hit them.

Gutierrez started fast with the Tigers, batting .299 after the first few weeks of the season. But just about everyone figured Cocoa was hitting over his head. By mid-June he had settled down to a more realistic .218 and managed to put together a particularly poor string of Sunday afternoon games—with 0 hits in 18 times at bat. Even Cocoa shouldn't have been too disappointed when Manager Mayo Smith benched him in favor of Ken Szotkiewicz for the first game of a Sunday doubleheader against the Cleveland Indians, June 21.

But when the right-handed-hitting Szotkiewicz went hitless in the opening game, the left-handed-hitting Gutierrez replaced him for the second game.

When Cocoa learned he would be batting against a young lefty Cleveland rookie, he brashly told his teammate, slugger Willie Horton, "Watch me get two hits."

Gutierrez got one of those two hits in the first inning when he looped a single to centerfield off his rookie opponent, Rick Austin. He also scored the Tigers' initial run. The next time he came to bat was in the third inning and again he tagged Austin for a single—this time a hard drive to centerfield—and again scored a run. It touched off a rally that helped the Tigers narrow the Indians' margin to 6-5 in what was developing into a wide-open game. After the second single, Horton wryly suggested to the little Venezuelan that he ought to get two more hits.

Gutierrez more than took Horton's advice. Cocoa pushed a drive into the hole between third and shortstop in the fifth inning against a new Cleveland pitcher and beat out the grounder for another single. In the seventh inning, he punched out a double. In the eighth, he swung his 36-ounce bat and connected solidly for a single that drove in a run to tie the game at 8-all. The tying run was an important one for Gutierrez; it would set him up for an opportunity to make history.

In the 20th Century, no major-league ballplayer had ever gotten seven consecutive hits in the same game. Others had had seven or more hits, but they were interspersed with outs, walks or hit-by-pitches.

The game went into extra innings when neither team scored in the ninth. So up came Gutierrez again, this time with a chance to join those players who had tied the major-league record of 6-for-6. He did, too, with a grounder through the middle of the infield which the Indian shortstop dove for and touched, but couldn't hold. The shortstop recovered the ball but couldn't get to second base in time to make the force-out on another Tiger runner, so Cocoa had hit No. 6. The Tigers' batting coach, Wally Moses, who had been working closely with Gutierrez during his slump, informed him that he had some kind of a record.

"I said I'll try for seven," said the surprised hitter, "but never in my life did I ever think of a record."

When both teams went scoreless in that inning and the next, Gutierrez was able to go for the record he hadn't known about.

Phil Hennigan, a Vietnam veteran, was on the mound for the Indians in the twelfth inning when the fledgling record-breaker came up for his final try. He was the fifth pitcher Gutierrez would face that Sunday. Tiger teammate Mickey Stanley had already put Detroit ahead, 9-8, with a homerun before Cocoa got to bat, relieving some of the pressure from him.

Hennigan was still upset by Stanley's shot hit over the centerfield fence. Gutierrez slammed the ball right at the pitcher. It was a hard drive that Gutierrez later said was his best-hit ball of the day. Hennigan got a glove on it, but could not hold it. He searched for the ball and tried to recover it as Gutierrez raced for first base. By the time Hennigan made his throw, Cocoa had arrived safely on first. There was no question about the drive being a clean hit. No. 7 had made his seventh hit in seven times at bat. Suddenly the No. 7 uniform he had been issued when he joined the Detroit Tigers had taken on a new meaning. The Tigers hung on to win the game.

In one game alone, Gutierrez had raised his batting average a full 31 points, from .218 to .249. He continued to start at shortstop for the Tigers after that in 1970, then lost his job in 1971 to a .228 hitter. Soon after, he was out of the majors.

The final irony of the story of No. 7 was that he only wore his lucky number by a fluke. In 1968, following the premature death of Tiger Manager Charlie Dressen, who wore No. 7, the number was temporarily retired. For no reason at all, it was brought out again by the equipment manager when Gutierrez joined the team.

*   *   *

One of baseball's only two other 7-for-7 days occurred before there even was an American League. It happened on June 10, 1892, when Baltimore had a National League franchise.

That day, in a game against St. Louis, the old Baltimore Orioles got hot and everybody but the pitcher was getting two or more hits. St. Louis' pitching staff was having a terrible day holding down the Baltimore bats, perhaps because one of its hurlers was a youngster making his first and only major-league appearance, and another was only a couple of years removed from the semi-pro ranks.

Baltimore had 25 runs by the end of the sixth inning.

Leading the Oriole attack was its catcher, Wilbert Robinson, an unimposing hitter batting eighth in the order. The short, robust Robinson, a lifetime .273 hitter, who later became manager of the Brooklyn Dodgers, found the range against St. Louis. He bopped six singles and a double in seven times at bat for the first and only 7-for-7 day until Gutierrez came along eight decades later. Unlike Gutierrez, Robinson collected his seven hits in nine innings.

Strangely enough, Robinson's feat went unnoticed for almost two decades. It wasn't until Robinson, by then a big-league manager, mentioned it to a sportswriter in 1912 that the record day was given any newspaper reviews. In 1892 it wasn't reported at all except in the box score.

The third member of the 7-for-7 club is Rennie Stennett of the Pittsburgh Pirates, a .274 career hitter over 11 major-league seasons. On September 16, 1975, his fifth year in the big leagues, he had four singles, two doubles and a triple in seven trips to the plate.

*   *   *

The most hits in a single game?

It happened in 1932, when shortstop John Burnett of the Cleveland Indians lashed out seven singles and two doubles in nine times at bat on July 10. However, the hits were not consecutive during the 18-inning game.

Like Gutierrez, Burnett played only one year as a major-league regular.

16 Consecutive Trips to the Plate— 16 Times on Base

Ted Williams had just passed his 39th birthday in late August of 1957, but he still was the most dangerous batter in baseball. That year the Boston Red Sox outfielder batted .388—the closest any major leaguer has come to hitting .400 since Williams himself achieved that figure in 1941.

But shortly after Williams reached age 39, he was forced to sit out a couple of weeks due to illness.

He was still too weak to play full time when he came back to the team on September 17. That didn't stop him from slugging a pinch-hit homerun, though.

The next day, Williams got into a game again as a pinch hitter and was walked. In his next pinch situation, he homered again.

Healthy enough to play full time again, he was back in the starting lineup on September 20. He celebrated his return by getting on base each time he went to bat. In the first of those at-bats he was walked. After homering the next time up, he was walked twice.

On September 22, he started again. And once more he got on base each time he went to bat. First came a walk, then a homerun (which gave him four straight homers in official at-bats). He singled his third time up, then was walked again. Williams had now reached base 11 straight times.

Even at 39, Williams remained the most feared batter in baseball, which was the reason for all the walks. In 1957 alone, he was intentionally walked 33 times for the official record (though Babe Ruth fans claim their man was passed intentionally as many as 80 times in a season).

On September 23, Williams was back on base again. He singled his first time up, then was walked three more times. In his fifth at-bat Williams was hit by a pitched ball.

He had come to bat 16 times since sitting out two weeks because of illness and each time he reached base successfully. It is a record that still stands. But then, Ted Williams was expected to set records that would stand the test of time.

*   *   *

Third baseman Tommy Brown of the Nashville Vols of the Southern Association probably holds the all-time professional record for getting on base in successive at-bats.

In May 1956, Brown had a string of 10 hits and six bases-on-balls before going into a game with the Birmingham Barons. The Barons chose to walk him four times rather than pitch to him—so Brown stretched his on-base streak to 20. His last time up, he flied out.

Seven .300 Hitters in Lineup, Team Finishes Last

Their batting order was imposing, and certainly one of the greatest ever in baseball for a single season. The 1930 Philadelphia Phillies often fielded a team with *seven* .300 hitters in the lineup at one time. And they weren't cheap .300 hitters, either.

In the outfield were Chuck Klein (.386), Lefty O'Doul (.383) and Don Hurst (.327) or Barney Friberg (.341). Third baseman Pinky Whitney batted .342 that year. Part-time first baseman Monk Sherlock, who shared his position with Hurst, batted .324. The platooning catchers, Harry McCurdy and Spud Davis, hit .331 and .313, respectively. Shortstop Tommy Thevenow batted .286 and his keystone mate, second baseman Fresco Thompson, hit .282. By today's standards, Thevenow and Thompson would gain the respect of the finest pitchers.

As a ballclub that season, the powerful Phillies averaged .315 at bat.

And what did such fine hitting get the Phillies?

Not much. That year, they finished a dead last in the eight-team National League—a full 40 games out of first place!

Seems that the '30 Phillies liked to give better than receive. Despite scoring 994 runs, the Phillies gave up a whopping 1,199 while losing 102 of 154 games.

There was an explanation for the Phillies' strange success/failure story. The National League had a hopped ball in play that season. Six of eight teams batted over .300 and the other two bettered the .280 mark. The league-leading St. Louis Cardinals alone had eleven .300 hitters and the New York Giants set the all-time major-league record by batting .319 as a unit. A 4.07 earned run average got a man fifth place in the National League pitching statistics.

The following season, the zip was taken out of the ball and no one in the National League batted over .350. No team batted over .289.

As for the Phillies in 1931? They fell off 36 points in team batting—and gained two notches in the standings.

*   *   *

The last of the .300-hitting teams was the 1950 Boston Red Sox of the American League. The Bosox, featuring Ted Williams (.317), Billy Goodman (.354), Dom

DiMaggio (.328), Al Zarilla (.325), Walt Dropo (.322) and others, averaged .302 for the season. Red Sox players crossed the plate over 1,000 times in 154 games.

And what did the Red Sox get for their efforts? A third-place finish in an eight-team league.

No Stroke of Genius

As a hitter, Ty Cobb had no peer, and his career average of .367, the best in baseball history, attests to the fact. As manager of the Detroit Tigers late in his career, however, he often was questioned and criticized. One decision he made in his final season as a player-manager could not be disputed, though. In 1926, Cobb batted .339, but he did not put himself in the lineup on a regular basis.

Instead, he went with an outfield of Harry Heilmann in rightfield, Heinie Manush in center and Bob (Fat) Fothergill in left. Heilmann and Fothergill hit .367 on the nose, and Manush won the American League batting title with .378.

Driving the Opposition Batty

The most runs-batted-in during a single game by a major leaguer is 12, a record established back in 1924 by the St. Louis Cardinals' cleanup batter, Jim Bottomley. Tony Lazzeri of the New York Yankees, another cleanup hitter, set the American League mark with 11, thanks to two grand slammers, in a 1936 game. And minor leaguers have gotten as many as 16 in a single contest.

• V •

Playing the Field

Always on the Job

When Cal Ripken, Jr. came up to the majors in a late-season call-up in 1981, the Baltimore Orioles figured they had their third baseman of the future. They knew that Ripken, son of one of the team's coaches, could hit for average and power and that he was an outstanding fielder.

And, with Cal, Jr. only just turned 21 years old, the Orioles figured they could count on him for some time.

Yet even the Orioles didn't figure they could count on young Ripken *all the time*.

On June 5 the following season, Ripken began one of the most startling strings in baseball history, one unmatched since Lou Gehrig stepped out of the New York Yankee lineup after playing 2,130 consecutive games in the 1920s and 1930s.

Ripken played every inning for six straight games at third base. Then he moved over to shortstop, where he continued to play every inning of every game—a streak that was going strong through the 1986 season.

He had played 765 consecutive regular-season games, nothing compared with Gehrig's record. But his other string of 6,947 consecutive innings without a break—and still counting—was unmatched in baseball history.

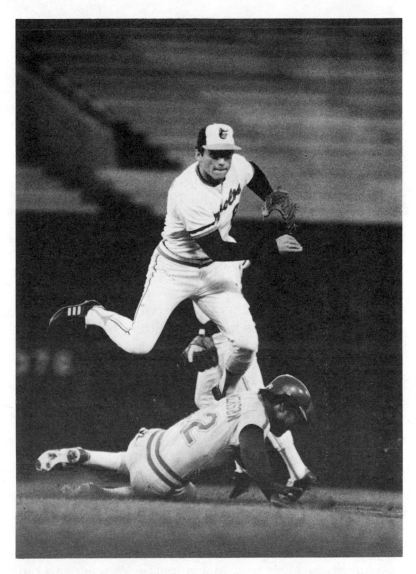

When Cal Ripken (throwing) reached the majors, he came to play—and did.

Ripken's mark drew the attention of statisticians, amateurs and pros, and no one could find a previous streak longer than the 534 games (the total innings weren't figured) that Buck Freeman had played for the Boston Red Sox, 1901-05, without coming out of a game.

The only time Ripken ever got to watch from the bench while his team was in the field was in All-Star Games, which like post-season games don't count against his streak. And Ripken being in All-Star Games was becoming a habit, too, in the 1980s.

Two Players with "Nine Lives"

Most baseball players enjoy the security of playing only one position. It's healthier for the batting average, they figure, and other times it's just healthier being adjusted to balls coming only from one direction.

But Bert Campaneris decided to be more daring than his big-league counterparts near the end of the 1965 American League campaign. The Kansas City A's were struggling along in last place, trying to evoke some interest before they moved on to a new home in Oakland, California. Throughout most of 1965, Campaneris, a spirited base runner, was all Kansas City had to cheer about.

As a rookie in 1964, Campaneris had played shortstop, third base and the outfield in an effort to establish a position. The 22-year-old Cuban was definitely big-league material. It was just a matter of where to put him so that he could go about the business of generating some offense.

By 1965, he was set at shortstop, where he would become outstanding.

But when the crowds dwindled late in the season, Campaneris and the A's' unconventional owner, Charley O. Finley, came up with a gimmick to draw some more fans. Campaneris would attempt to become the first man in modern baseball history to play every position—and do it in one game.

Finley took out a million-dollar insurance policy on Campaneris for September 8. Then Campy Campaneris Night was proclaimed publicly, and Finley took advertisements in local newspapers to bellow out Campaneris' bold adventurous attempt. It was rumored that Finley also slipped Campaneris a few extra dollars for the announced attraction.

Campaneris deserved it. Over 21,000 fans came to the game at Kansas City's Municipal Stadium to see if Campy could play all nine positions against the California Angels.

Campaneris opened the game at his usual position—shortstop. He didn't field a ball.

In the next inning he moved to second base and got an assist when he ran down a trapped baserunner.

In Inning No. 3, Campy played third and didn't have to budge.

Then he moved to each of the outfield positions for innings 4, 5 and 6. He caught fly balls in left and center but dropped a wind-blown fly in right that cost the A's a run. He was charged with an error.

In the seventh inning, Campaneris moved to first base. At 5 feet 10 inches and 160 pounds, he hardly could compare with the tall, well-built sluggers who usually get that chore. But he held his own and caught an infield popup.

It was over to the pitching mound in the eighth inning of what had developed into a tight 2-1 game, the

Angels leading. But Campy got his cousin, José Cardenal, out on a pop fly. However, he walked the next two men on eight straight pitches, then got nipped for a single that drove in a run. He did strike out Bobby Knoop, a .269 hitter. And he got out of the inning with no further damage when a baserunner was thrown out trying to steal.

Offensively, Campaneris went hitless. He picked up his 49th steal of the year and scored a run after a walk in the first inning. But then he wasn't out to prove anything on offense that night.

The biggest test, according to Campaneris, came in the ninth when he moved in behind the plate to catch. That's why he saved it for last.

The first man up for the Angels, 200-pound Ed Kirkpatrick, singled and stole second on Campaneris. The next man walked and the following player flied out with Kirkpatrick moving to third.

With a man on first and third, the Angels decided to try a double steal on the raw recruit behind the plate. Campaneris threw to his second baseman, Dick Green, who quickly relayed the ball back home to catch the charging Kirkpatrick. Campaneris took Green's throw while he was standing a few feet in front of the plate on the third base side. Kirkpatrick had only one chance—to knock the ball out of Campaneris' hands. So he barreled into him and knocked him to the ground. Campaneris bravely held onto the ball for the out. Then, like a good tough catcher, he went to battle Kirkpatrick with his fists.

The insurance company got a slight scare out of the ordeal, because Campaneris was carted off to a local hospital for X-rays of his shoulder. But he proved to be okay.

Cesar Tovar of the Minnesota Twins was almost better suited for the same record attempt in 1968. He had played six different positions in the big leagues, the only ones he hadn't tried beforehand being pitcher, catcher and first base. And he had played the other six positions extensively, depending on where manager Cal Ermer had needed him.

A good hitter, Tovar didn't seem to be bothered by switching around, though he once said he would prefer rightfield if he had a choice.

By September 1968, he had switched positions some 40 times during the season. And he made only three errors. At bat, the little 155-pound Venezuelan kept his average in the .280 range.

So on September 22, he was prepared for a nine-position night. The opposing team was the Oakland A's—featuring Bert Campaneris.

Tovar bravely started out on the mound. The first man he faced was, appropriately, Bert Campaneris. Tovar got him out on a foul ball to third. Next came powerful Reggie Jackson. Tovar struck him out after a full count. Danny Cater walked and went to second on a balk, but Tovar survived the inning by getting Sal Bando to foul out.

Tovar proudly wore a jacket on the walk in from the bullpen, as all pitchers do, and made use of the resin bag. He did suffer from a sore arm the next day, though, and it was directly attributed to his no-hit pitching stint.

Next inning, Tovar was behind the plate in another show of strength. His equipment wasn't up to par, but he held onto a third strike, kept two base runners in check, and even made a trip to the mound to confer with his pitcher.

From then on, Tovar went around the horn—playing

first, second, short and third for an inning each. There were no disasters. He had an assist at first and a putout at second. Then came the outfield positions that were natural to him. He made two catches in left and one in center. All in all, he handled six chances, handled them well, and retired as a no-hit pitcher. Bert Campaneris was proud of him.

Records Are Made to Break

With the knowledge of the Campaneris-Tovar record in mind, Mike Ashman of the minor-league Albany-Colonie A's parlayed an advantage he had over the former major leaguers one day in 1983.

In a June 4 game against Nashua, an Eastern League foe, Ashman started out as the team's designated hitter, a position not yet invented when Campaneris and Tovar proved their versatility. Ashman went on to play the other nine positions, too, thus becoming the first player to play all 10 positions in one game.

Unassisted Triple Play in World Series

The fans at the Cleveland Indian-Brooklyn Dodger World Series game on October 10, 1920, were being treated to more than their share of Series history. Indian rightfielder Elmer Smith smacked a grand-slam homerun in the first inning—the first such slam in Series history. Then Indian pitcher Jim Bagby slugged one out of the park in the third inning to become the first pitcher to get a four-bagger in Series play. The game was becoming a rout, much to the pleasure of the hometown Indian fans. As it turned out, the Dodgers would out-hit the Indians that day, 13-12, and still lose, 8-1.

But the best fireworks of the game were still to come. In the fifth inning, the Dodgers started getting to Bagby, a 31-game winner that season. There were no outs and two men on—Otto Miller on first and Pete Kilduff on second—when Clarence Mitchell came to bat for Brooklyn in the fifth. Mitchell was a pretty good hitting pitcher who had come in to relieve the Dodger starter just the inning before.

Bill Wambsganss was settled in his second-base position as the husky left-handed Mitchell dug in at the plate to face Jim Bagby.

Then it happened— "All in a flash," recalled Wambsganss, a veteran infielder who lasted 13 years in the majors because of his catlike defense.

Mitchell drove a hard liner toward right-center. Luckily for Wambsganss, it came right at his head. Kilduff and Miller took off like a shot at the crack of the bat; to them, it could not have seemed like anything but a long hit.

But Wambsganss speared the drive out of the air as the baserunners raced head, down to try to score.

Wambsganss rushed to second, where he retired Kilduff by stepping on the base he had just left. By now, Miller was nearing second and had not yet grasped the situation. For some reason, Miller kept coming at Wambsganss instead of making the turn and trying to get back to first. So Wambsganss tagged him out.

He had performed baseball's rare *unassisted* triple play under World Series conditions. Within a matter of five or six seconds, the weak-hitting second baseman with a flair for fielding had etched his name into baseball's archives.

Wambsganss often reminded others that he could have missed his coveted spot in history.

"A few feet one way or another and it would have been a safe hit," he said. "It came to me like a shot, high in the air, so I reached for it, grabbed it and held it. As for Miller, he could have turned. He wouldn't have made it, but he would have caused me to throw (to first) and lose the unassisted triple play."

There have been only eight unassisted triple plays in big-league history—five by shortstops and two by first basemen. All came with men on first and second. Wambsganss was the only second baseman ever to make the astonishing play.

But according to Wambsganss, a second baseman just missed on another occasion. The near-miss performer was Wambsganss himself.

He told of the time, in a game against the old St. Louis Browns, when he speared a line drive, tagged out a man who had just left second, and then began to chase down a slow-footed Brownie who was headed back to first base. Wambsganss ran after him until the final moment, then felt obligated to make the throw to nail the runner.

Were there ever back-to-back triple plays in consecutive innings? Yes, but it wasn't Tinkers-to-Evers-to-Chance, and it wasn't in the majors, either.

Heffner-to-somebody-to-somebody got lost in history. But the Welch, W. Va., Miners of the Appalachian League had a combination that for one day outdid the old Chicago Cub threesome.

In the seventh inning of a July 26, 1954, game against Johnson City, third baseman Lee Heffner scooped up a grounder with runners on first and second and tagged the base in front of him for a quick out. Then he tossed the ball to his second baseman for another out and the second sacker tossed it to first for the triple play.

That wasn't uncommon, but when Heffner snared a line drive in the next inning and threw the ball to second, and the second baseman relayed it on to first for another triple play, the Welch Miners had dug out a feat that may never have been achieved before.

Outfielder's Triple Play

Only eight unassisted triple plays have occurred in big-league baseball and few are accomplished in the minors.

But Walter Carlisle of the Vernon team (based in Los Angeles) of the Pacific Coast League added a footnote to fielding history during a game played July 19, 1911. Vernon was playing the Los Angeles club.

With the score tied in the ninth inning, and men on first and second with none out, Los Angeles signaled for the hit-and-run.

As the Los Angeles batter swung, Carlisle edged in from his position in centerfield until he was almost at second base.

In one of the quickest swoops ever seen on a baseball field, Carlisle grabbed a line drive, somersaulted, landed on his feet, tagged second base for Out No. 2, then ran to first base before the baserunner could get back for Out No. 3.

Carlisle, a centerfielder, had performed a feat no

Dale Long (left) was the first lefty in the majors since 1902 to perform behind the plate (1958) and 22 years later (1980) Mike Squires (right) of the White Sox tried catching for several games.

other professional baseball player ever had—an unassisted triple play by an outfielder!

Lest some other outfielder thinks he can match Carlisle's feat, he must remember that there was something special about him—he was an ex-circus acrobat.

Left-Handed Catchers in the Majors

It was the second or third day of spring practice in San Bernardino, Calif., for the Pittsburgh Pirates in 1951 when Manager Billy Meyer approached rookie first baseman Dale Long to inform him that the team's general manager, Branch Rickey, wanted to try him out as a catcher. Long was game for the experiment—"I'd have done anything, even run through brick walls, to make the majors," he said—but he felt he should remind the manager of one thing: he was a left-handed thrower. Meyer's initial reaction was to take out a copy of the roster with its pertinent physical characteristics and read it in front of Long.

"By God, you *are* a lefty," said Meyer.

Before sending Long behind the plate, Meyer felt obligated to contact Rickey, an ex-catcher himself, and let him know the surprising information he had just learned. The astute Rickey's answer was typical: "Judas Priest, Billy, that's what I want—a left-handed catcher."

Rickey, the pioneer who had introduced vast farm systems and the first black player, Jackie Robinson, to organized baseball, tried in 1951 to introduce the first left-handed catcher to the majors in modern times.

Long was a fast, homerun-hitting 25-year-old with impressive size. He was 6 feet, 4 inches tall and weighed about 200 pounds. Why Rickey singled him out for the experiment, Long never knew. But he gave it his best.

Each day, he'd get up earlier than the other players and catch 200 balls tossed at him by Iron Mike, the pitching machine. Long had a morning companion—a young player Rickey was trying to switch from a right-handed batter to a lefty. The prospect had struck out 195 times the previous season.

They made an odd couple. Long would work all morning with Iron Mike and his wild-swinging human companion, play four or five innings of an exhibition game behind the plate, then return to the pitching machine for more practice late in the afternoon. But the great experiment fizzled and Long never did catch for the Pirates. He went on to earn his fame in another fashion, slugging home runs in eight straight games as a first baseman.

"I kept a left-handed catcher's mitt around, though," he recalled. But the only use it got was in the dugout where Dale used it as a cushion.

Then one day in 1958, when he didn't have his special mitt anymore, Long was summoned to catch. He was playing for the Chicago Cubs that season. Cal Neeman, the Cubs' regular catcher, was ejected from the game. His backup had pinch hit earlier in the day, so he too was out of the game. Manager Bob Scheffing pleaded with the umpire, but to no avail. "That's your problem," he was told.

Scheffing, an ex-catcher, apparently had heard of the Long experiment. He called on his slugging first baseman to fill in behind the plate that August day against the Philadelphia Phillies. Long donned all the catching gear except for a mitt. He had to use his first baseman's glove.

Long toiled behind the plate for the rest of that inning plus another one. Despite the lack of glove and preparation, there were no major disasters. But the next day, a Cub representative was dispatched to the Chicago-based Wilson Sporting Goods Company to purchase an emergency supply of left-handed catcher's mitts. A month later, in another emergency situation against the Los Angeles Dodgers, Long filled in for a short stretch and again avoided any catastrophes.

Why hadn't there been other left-handed catchers?

Probably because there have been no other Branch Rickeys. Baseball is wedded to its traditions and a left-handed catcher is just too much to get used to.

For Dale Long, there were some definite problems. Many of them had to do with pitchers not being able to adjust. The hurlers just could not get used to the vision of a catcher's mitt protruding from the opposite side of the plate.

Years later, however, Long admitted there were some personal areas of difficulty as well. "We really do live in a right-hander's world," he said. For some reason that he couldn't explain—and he was a pretty good student of the game—it was more difficult for a left-hander to make the throw to second base. He said that the lefty's throw had a sideways spin that made it "sail" during the 127-foot toss. Because the throw drifted away from second, Long had to make adjustments.

His toughest situation, however, was an opponent stealing third when a right-handed pitcher was on the mound and a left-handed batter was at the plate. "You had to turn your whole body away from the movement when that happened," he recalled.

As for stepping in behind the plate in an emergency, Long had no real problem with signs. "I just used the 1-2-3 system," he said. "One finger for a fastball, two for a curve, three for a change of speed and I wiggled one for a changeup." Making history was as simple as that.

*   *   *

In 1980, baseball got its second left-handed catcher in more than three-quarters of a century. Mike Squires, who had played 122 games for the Chicago White Sox at several positions in 1979, was trying to find a way to stay in the majors at age 28. Squires had had a conversation with the team's vice president, Rollie Hemond, who had mentioned that one of the quickest ways to get to the majors would be as a left-handed catcher. Hemond sounded serious.

Squires volunteered to give it a try in 1980, as long as the White Sox were serious, and not just using it as a gimmick to attract fans. Hemond got Squires a special-order left-handed mitt, and Squires used it in some intrasquad games.

Nothing else happened for a couple of months until Squires suggested to his manager that he be given a chance to catch in case an emergency arose when the team was desperate for an experienced catcher.

Squires got his chance, for one inning, on May 4 against the Milwaukee Brewers. He caught the ball well, and also called such good pitches that the hurler shook him off only once in 14 pitches. He got another chance to catch a few days later against the Kansas City Royals, and again he caught a scoreless inning.

But baseball was not ready for a lefty behind the plate full time, or even as a starter. That didn't keep Squires from prolonging his career. The versatile athlete also pitched a game in 1984 and played more than a dozen games as one of the few left-handed third basemen in the game's history.

Rifle Arms

Baseball scouts get fascinated by the throwing arms of the prospects they are checking out. But players are careful not to test their arms for distance throwing too often, for fear of injury.

Throughout the years, though, some players have taken up the challenge to see just who is the longest distance thrower. For years, that distinction belonged to an ex-minor leaguer named Sheldon LeJeune. In an exhibition at Cincinnati in 1910, LeJeune tossed a ball 426 feet, 9½ inches. He had just completed his season with Evansville of the Central League.

LeJeune saw his record stand for 42 years. It wasn't until September 7, 1952, that another minor leaguer—Don Grate, who played for Chattanooga of the Southern Association—outdistanced him. Grate threw a ball 434 feet, 1 inch. But even Grate's mark was not out of reach for another rifle arm—ex-big league outfielder Glen Gorbous.

Gorbous had played briefly and without distinction with the Cincinnati Reds and Philadelphia Phillies in 1955 and 1956. The lanky 6-foot-2-inch Canadian just wasn't up to major-league standards as a hitter. But he could throw. He proved that in the 1957 season when he played for a minor-league team in Omaha of the American Association.

In a pre-planned exhibition on August 1, Gorbous made four throws from the rightfield corner at Omaha Stadium to the leftfield corner. For each attempt, he would get a six-step running start. Aided by a slight 3-mph tailwind, Gorbous made one throw that was measured at 445 feet, 10 inches. It's still the record to beat.

Catching from On High

Babe Ruth and Gabby Street were two baseball players who reached their peaks in big-league games. But the real "height" of their careers came off the field. In fact, Street probably got more notoriety from an off-field antic than he ever did for his fine catching with the Washington Senators.

On the morning of August 21, 1908, Street went out to the Washington Monument. He would attempt what would be a monumental catch—a baseball dropped from the top of that landmark. Street's friend, Preston Gibson, had made a $500 bet that the Senator catcher could catch a ball dropped from the 555-foot-high window at the top of the monument. Gibson and his challenger ascended to the top of the structure with a basket full of baseballs and a wooden chutelike device that would send the balls sailing off away from the side. Street was at the ground level, waiting for their first drop.

Gibson sent ten balls down the chute in his quest to give Street a fair chance. But none seemed to clear the side of the monument, which is an obelisk, wider at the bottom than at the top. So the chute was put aside and Gibson started throwing the balls out of the little window. Three throws later, Street scrambled around on the ground and made his historic catch. He admitted later that he couldn't see the balls until they were halfway down. He also said the wind hindered him.

Scientists have estimated that the ball had a force of some 200 to 300 pounds at the time Street got a mitt on it.

Though Street got most of the publicity for making a high catch, he wasn't the only person to reach such heights. Thirty years later, two Cleveland Indian catchers—Frankie Pytlak and Hank Helf—caught balls dropped from the 710-foot level of Terminal Tower in Cleveland.

Another Cleveland player, Joe Sprinz, performed the greatest stunt catch, though, when he took in a ball dropped 800 feet from an airship in 1931. The record-holder paid for his catch: the force of the catch broke his jaw.

The Baseball Hall of Fame in Cooperstown, N.Y. was surprised to receive some rare Babe Ruth photos in the 1970s. One photo showed the Babe chasing around in an open field in an attempt to get a ball dropped from a double-winged plane. Legend has it that the Babe made the catch.

The common thinking now is that ballplayers shouldn't try such freak stunts because it isn't worth the risk to their well-paid careers.

Babe Ruth circling around, trying to catch a ball dropped from the plane above.

• VI •
Age Gaps

Oldsters

When Phil Niekro completed a game for the Yankees at age 46 in 1985, it was pointed out that he was the oldest pitcher to do so. But he was a mere youngster compared with Satchel Paige, who pitched his last game at age 59. In 1965, Charley Finley, then the owner of the Kansas City Athletics, had brought back Paige, a star of the Negro Leagues who didn't make his major-league debut until 1948, for one last fling. Paige justified his appearance by going three shutout innings against the Boston Red Sox, giving up only one hit and even recording a strikeout.

With some help from Lloyd Johnson, a former researcher for the Baseball Hall of Fame, and the recently released sixth edition of "The Baseball Encyclopedia," which has revised some birthdates of old-timers, here are how players at other positions have solved the age-old problem:

Catcher: Jim O'Rourke, born in 1852, was the first man to come to bat in National League history. He retired in 1893, after having played every position, but mostly the outfield, for 18 years. Then he came back in 1904 to catch a game for the New York Giants when he was 52. The rest must have done him good: he got a hit.

Age did not hold back Satchel Paige (left). Warren Spahn (right) turned his no-hit games into his personal "Old-Timers' Days."

First base: Hughie Jennings occasionally put himself in the Detroit Tiger lineup after he became manager in 1905 at 38. The last time he did it was in 1918, when he was 49.

Second base: Arlie Latham stole 129 bases one year in a 17-season major-league career interspersed from

1880-1909. In his final year, at age 50, Latham played four games at second for the New York Giants and stole a base.

Third base: Jimmy Austin, who was born in Wales, got a late start in his career, not reaching the majors until 1909, when he was 29. He pretty much retired in 1922, but caught his only major league game in 1923, and played one game each at third in 1925, 1926 and finally, at age 49, in 1929.

Shortstop: Bobby Wallace played 25 straight years in the majors, and his last game at short in 1918 was as a St. Louis Cardinal, when he was 44.

Outfield: Sam Thompson, who had begun his career with Detroit in the National League in 1885, was brought back in 1906, eight years after his retirement, to boost attendance for the fledgling American League Tigers. Then 46, he played eight games in the outfield, and had a triple among his 7 hits. Sam Rice, playing 78 games in the field in 1934 for the Cleveland Indians after 19 years with the Washington Senators, was 44 when he called it quits. In 1983, in the last day of a 23-year career, Carl Yastrzemski of the Boston Red Sox played two games in left, also at 44.

Designated hitter: at 53, Minnie Minoso returned to the Chicago White Sox for three games in 1976 and got a hit in eight trips at bat.

Pinch-hitter: Minoso came back once again in 1980, tying Nick Altrock's record as the only man to play in five different decades. He also bettered by months Altrock's mark of being the oldest man to go to the plate, both being 57. Altrock, mainly a pitcher (and a comedian), had done it in 1933 for the Washington Senators.

Manager: This one took little research. Connie Mack managed the Philadelphia Athletics in 1950, at age 87.

Late but Great

Thirty-nine is an age when most major-league baseball players are retired. But when pitcher Warren Spahn reached that milestone in 1960 the only retiring he was doing was to enemy batsmen. At 39, Spahn was not merely going strong, he was going very strong.

The season was coming to a close on September 16 when the Milwaukee Braves were scheduled to pitch Spahn against the hapless, last-place Philadelphia Phillies. It would be a good opportunity for Spahn to pick up his 20th victory for the fifth year in a row. That is, if he hadn't lost his fastball—as some newspaper accounts had indicated. Undoubtedly, the critics were influenced by his slow start. He was only 4-4 in late June.

In fact, lanky Warren Spahn had been a late starter in the big leagues. He pitched a dozen or so innings for the old Boston Braves in 1942 but did not earn a decision. That had to wait until 1946, when he came back from World War II. Spahn was 25 before he got his first major-league victory. Contrast that with a pitcher like Dennis McLain, who had already reached the 100-victory mark at age 25.

Spahn may have started late but his records are many. A fiercely competitive player who once posted a 23-7 record after tearing his knee cartilage in spring training, Spahn is regarded by many as the greatest left-handed pitcher of all time. In 1960 he was going after his 11th season with 20 or more victories and no one was about to stop him.

But for all his records, Spahn had never thrown a no-hitter in the majors. That was an omission for a man with 286 victories up to that time.

Was it a jinx?

Spahn apparently didn't think so.

On September 16, before the second smallest crowd in Milwaukee's major-league history, Spahn went to the mound and began making up for lost time.

He set down one Phillie after another, and surprisingly with a blazing fastball. He was throwing few pitches and very few balls. It was obvious to the 6,117 fans who did show up that he had his stuff this night.

In the fifth inning, Spahn decided to lessen the tension that was beginning to build. As he returned to the dugout after setting down the Phils in order, he said loud enough for his teammates to hear, "All right, just nobody say I got a no-hitter going." He smiled.

Spahn kept pitching flawless baseball, inning after inning. Going into the ninth inning, he hadn't even been ruffled by a Phillie hitter. He had only given up two walks and his strikeout count was reaching his personal best for nine innings.

The first two batters in the final inning were pinch hitters. Spahn disposed of them and collected his 15th strikeout—a personal high in a regulation-length game.

Then came his first challenge of the night.

Bob Malkmus, an infielder with a nondescript batting history, stretched Spahn to the full count. Then on a seventh pitch, Malkmus lined a drive straight at Spahn. Warren got a glove on it through pure luck, then lost the ball when it trickled away. As Spahn searched the infield for the ball, shortstop Johnny Logan raced in, picked up the ball and tossed it to first. Fortunately, Joe Adcock, a 6-foot-4-inch man, was playing first. He needed all the stretch he could manage to take Logan's low, wide throw. Adcock made a backhanded stab at the ball and got it in time.

Warren Spahn finally had his no-hitter. Never had a player so old accomplished so much in nine big-league innings.

Spahn's record didn't last for long, though. About six months later, a 40-year-old left-hander pitching against the San Francisco Giants only five days after his birthday hurled a no-hit game. Warren Spahn had done it again.

Spahn's ageless performances didn't end with the second no-hitter. He continued to win until he reached 363 victories, then went to the minor leagues at age 45 to try for a comeback. Along with his no-hitters, his other great late accomplishment came in 1963 when he was 42. That year, Spahn won 23 games and pitched seven shutouts, both matching his personal bests as a big leaguer. It was the 13th time he had won 20 games or more.

Junior High to Majors—in One Step

Major-league baseball didn't have a big-league look about it in 1944. Most of the bright young players were off to war, and baseball had to settle for the leftovers. Of 400 major-leaguers that year, some 157 of them were classified 4-F (physical rejects) by the United States military forces. Many others who filled up big-league rosters were old men—or teenagers.

Typical of the desperate teams was Cincinnati. The Reds were in the National League pennant race early in the season, but were losing players left and right to the military. The Reds, like other teams, were grabbing anybody who could move and putting him on the roster. Scouts were combing the sandlot leagues for instant major-league players.

When Joe Nuxhall put on his spikes for the first time in the majors at age 15, he made history.

It was on one such scouting trip to Hamilton, Ohio, that the Reds' scout found a strong-armed youngster named Joe Nuxhall. Actually, the scout had made the trip to Hamilton to take a look at Joe's father. He came away more impressed by the boy. Joe Nuxhall's father had been grooming the son for baseball for years. The father used to have the youngster throw chunks of coal at a spot on a silo after they unloaded trucks.

"I could throw hard," said Nuxhall about his early pitching. "But I didn't know where it was going."

In June 1944, "it" was going right to the major-leagues.

Nuxhall was just a junior-high-school student—15 years old. But the Reds offered him $500 to sign a contract and salary of $175 a month, and he grabbed it.

On June 10—when Joe was 15 years, 10 months and 11 days old—he found himself pitching against the league-leading St. Louis Cardinals at Cincinnati's Crosley Field.

Nuxhall had been brought right into the majors along with an 18- and a 19-year-old. Manager Bill McKechnie was hard-pressed for pitchers, so he was willing to look at anyone who could throw the ball. The lean left-handed teenager fit that category.

The Cardinals were leading in the June 10 game, 7-0, when McKechnie pulled his starter, a youngster he had just brought up from the Syracuse farm team on trial (the youngster lasted two days). McKechnie replaced him with a third baseman who had been converted into a pitcher. As the game progressed, the ex-third baseman didn't fare too well, either. He too was replaced, when the score reached 13-0. The manager summoned Nuxhall.

"I though Mr. McKechnie was kidding," the boyish pitcher recalled. So did the 3,500 fans. But he wasn't.

Nuxhall was visibly shaken when he reached the mound. But somehow he got the first batter to ground out, shortstop to first. He walked the next man, then threw a wild pitch while in the process of getting the third batter to pop out.

Then the roof fell in.

Nuxhall walked another batter, gave up a single, and walked three more. Runs were pouring across the plate and the Reds were heading for the worst defeat by a major-league team in nearly 40 years. Joe got the ninth batter he faced to a 3-2 count, then lost him with a single.

He had given up four runs and had men on base when he was replaced.

The Reds eventually lost, 18-0.

Nuxhall went back to high school after that and became a star athlete in basketball and football. But he continued in professional baseball, too.

The road back to the majors was a tough one for Nuxhall. There were stopovers at several minor-league towns, a series of temper tantrums to overcome and a control problem. One season in the minors, he walked 151 batters in 186 innings. But the Reds stood patiently behind him and in 1952 he rejoined the team. He was now 24 years old.

Nuxhall went on to play 15 more years in the majors, all but one with the Reds. He finished with 135 victories and a 3.90 earned run average overall. The career ERA was a marked improvement over that first season in the majors. After his two thirds of an inning in that first game against the Cardinals, he had posted a 67.50 ERA.

Fifteen years after his disastrous start at Crosley Field, Nuxhall found himself in another bases-loaded situation. He was pitching again at Crosley, this time against the Milwaukee Braves. In one inning, with the bases loaded Nuxhall fanned dangerous Eddie Mathews and Joe Adcock. Then when he struck out Del Crandall, another slugger, his catcher dropped the ball. Crandall made it to first base to load the bases.

This time, Nuxhall held his cool. The next man up was Johnny Logan. Nuxhall struck him out, too—giving him a rare four-strikeout inning. Only two other pitchers before Nuxhall had accomplished the feat in the 20th Century.

Recent research by the Baseball Hall of Fame in

Cooperstown, N.Y., indicates that Nuxhall may not have been the youngest major leaguer after all. A player named Fred Chapman took part in a game in 1887 for Philadelphia of the American Association, which was then a major league. Chapman's birthdate has been recorded as November 25, 1872, which would have made him only 14 years old during the summer of 1887.

But the very youngest player ever to take part in a professional game may have been 12-year-old Joe Relford, of Statesboro, Ga. It happened in 1952.

The fans hollered to the visiting Fitzgerald team, "Put in the batboy!" and manager Charlie Ridgeway obliged. His team was down 13-0 and playing terrible ball in the eighth inning. Ridgeway got the go-ahead from the umpire and inserted Relford in the lineup. First he pinch hit, grounding hard to third base, then took his position in centerfield. Relford made a fine stab of a long line drive during the game. For good measure, Joe Relford, who was black, automatically integrated the Class D Georgia State League for the first time.

The incident didn't go over well in the league office. The manager was suspended, the umpire fired, and the batboy dismissed.

14-Year-Old Pro

The scheduled 7:30 P.M. minor-league baseball game between Auburn and Batavia in the New York-Penn League had to be moved up to 6 P.M. on August 10, 1974, due to unforeseen circumstances. The hometown Auburn, N.Y., Phillies didn't want to get into trouble with the law.

What Auburn was being careful about was the New

York State child labor laws. The statutes read that an employee under 16 years could not work after 7 P.M. At the time, Auburn was trying to work 14-year-old Jorge Lebron into his first professional game, a debut that would make history. Lebron, a shortstop from Puerto Rico, was about to become the youngest player ever to sign a contract and participate in organized baseball.

The 5-foot-10-inch, 150-pounder eventually did play, and he certainly didn't embarrass the people who took a chance on him. On the first pitch of the game, a Batavia player smacked the ball down the middle of the infield. Lebron dashed over, scooped it off the ground and made a successful long throw to first base. He looked like a real pro. Lebron made another assist, a putout and drew a walk as leadoff man for his team during a three-inning stint.

Lebron had signed with the Philadelphia Phillie farm club in July after a scout in Puerto Rico spotted him and convinced the Phillies to take a chance on him, despite his age. Because Puerto Rican players do not fall within the framework of the major-league player draft, Lebron signed as a free agent. The general manager of the Auburn club was designated the teenager's legal guardian.

Lebron starred in his second game, too. Though he went hitless in four trips to the plate, he made a shoestring catch of one blooper and snagged a line drive, to the delight of 3,642 fans who packed into Auburn's 3,500-seat stadium for a game against Newark. Ironically, Auburn lost the game on errors in extra innings—long after the slick-fielding Lebron left the game.

Lebron's brief 1974 season came to an end after that game. He had to return to Puerto Rico to enroll in junior high school.

Young Major Leaguers

Some of the best youthful performances in big-league baseball include:

Al Kaline of the Detroit Tigers won a batting championship in the American League in 1955 when he was only 20. Kaline had over 200 hits and batted .340 that season. He never did that well again, ironically, in his 23-year career.

Freddie Lindstrom of the old New York Giants participated in a World Series game in 1924 when he was only 18 years, 10 months and 13 days "old."

Lou Boudreau of the Cleveland Indians took over as manager of his team in 1942 when he was only 24 years old. He continued to star as shortstop too, and at age 30 led the Indians to a World Series triumph.

Bobo Holloman of the St. Louis Browns made his first big-league start in 1953 his best one—he pitched a no-hitter against the Philadelphia Athletics. Holloman rarely pitched well after that.

Grover Cleveland Alexander of the Philadelphia Phillies won 28 games in his rookie year, 1911.

George Watkins of the St. Louis Cardinals batted .373 as a rookie in 1930.

Wally Berger of the Boston Braves in 1930 and Frank Robinson of the Cincinnati Reds in 1956, each hit 38 homers as rookies.

His Second Pro Game—a No-Hitter

Mickey Mattiace got off to a fast start in his first ten days as a professional baseball pitcher. The 20-year-old New Yorker, pitching for Palatka in the Florida State League, beat Daytona Beach on a no-hitter in his second pro game in April, 1960. He won his next start, then followed it up with another no-hitter against Tampa.

In just ten days as a pro, he had two no-hitters and a third victory.

Before the season was over, Mattiace added two more one-hitters to his impressive portfolio.

Player Pays to Get into Ballpark

Joe Carolan, a 21-year-old Detroiter, had enough confidence in his baseball ability to venture down to Columbus, Ga., in the spring of 1954 to seek a tryout with the minor-league Cardinals of that city.

The burly, 230-pounder got his tryout all right, but not until he paid his way into the ballpark and asked to speak to the Columbus manager.

The manager took one look at Carolan's size and learned about his determination. So he offered to let the Detroiter take batting practice with his team. Carolan knocked three balls out of the park during the drills. The manager responded by offering him a contract.

Carolan played that same day against the Macon team he had paid to see play.

On his first time up, in the first inning, Joe Carolan got his first hit as a professional. A grand-slam home run, naturally.

• VII •
Touching All Bases

Going Home in Record Time

Man is moving much faster in sports nowadays than he was in 1931. For example, the record for the 100-yard dash in track was then 9.6 seconds, more than a half second slower than modern sprinters can run. Yet no man has since circled the bases in baseball faster than Evar Swanson did in '31.

The "Swift Swede" was a 170-pound, all-around sports star, who once won 16 letters at Lombard (Ill.) College and played four years of professional football as well as making it to the major leagues as an outfielder. Swanson was a pretty good major-leaguer, with a lifetime batting average over .300 for 515 games, but he played in an era when the pay was not particularly high. The most Swanson ever made was $8,500.

To compensate, athletes of that time used to go barnstorming in the off-season or take part in special promotions during regular-season games, such as fungo hitting contests, throwing for distance, etc. Getting timed for circling the bases was another favorite—and Swanson's specialty.

Swanson took part in one such promotion during a Cincinnati game on September 15, 1929. His competition included his fleet teammate, Ethan Allen, and the Boston Braves' Lance Richbourg. Each man would have one try, lining up like a sprinter behind home plate and then dashing around the bases, touching each one, before crossing the plate. The minimum distance for the run is 120 yards.

Another Cincinnati player, Hans Lobert, had set the unofficial big-league record at 13.8 seconds in 1910. Swanson was in the midst of his best major-league season, one in which he would steal 33 bases to finish second in the National League, so he was a top candidate to challenge Lobert's old mark.

With a $75 prize offered by the ballclub, there was even more incentive than pride.

After Allen and Richbourg made their runs, Swanson went into his trackman's start and waited for the signal to dash off toward first. When he got it, he raced fast and intelligently, careful to tag the inside of each base and not waste time by taking wide turns at the bases.

Stopwatches in 1929 were manually operated and clocked runners to fifths of a second instead of tenths, so Swanson reached home in 13.4 seconds, completely smashing the old mark. A later look at the timing device indicated he was closer to 13.3; but the 13.4 stood.

Two years later, on September 20, 1931, the stopwatches were divided into tenths of seconds. That year, before a game at Columbus, O., Swanson got his 13.3 officially. The record has never been bettered. George Case, a great baserunner for the Washington Senators, came closest, clocking 13.5 in 1943. Mickey Rivers, an outfielder for the California Angels, attempted the feat in 1971 and could do only 14.3 He found out what many fleet candidates did—that it takes more than speed.

Signed Big-League Contract
Before Ever Playing a Game

The Cincinnati Reds were holding a tryout camp in 1947 on one of the wide-open ranges of Texas when a scraggly teenager showed up. The player had never participated in a baseball game before, and at age 16 hardly seemed like much of a prospect. But the manager of the Bonham, Texas, softball team suggested that his star shortstop, 5-foot-11-inch, 160-pound Roy McMillan, go over to Tyler, Texas, and attend the Reds' camp.

Tryout camps were fairly open in those days and big-league teams were generous in giving anyone a quick look-see before inviting the outstanding prospects back for more sessions.

They liked what they saw in the youthful McMillan as he scooted around the infield like a waterbug, scooping ground balls out of the dirt and stabbing line drives in the air. McMillan, who would earn the nickname "Radar" in coming years for his ability to trace the baseball in the field, was offered a contract. He was signed for $250.

McMillan began to play almost immediately for the Reds' farm club in Ballinger, Texas, of the Lone Star State League. He moved swiftly up the ranks—to Tyler, Tex.; Columbia, S.C.; and Tulsa, Okla., one step each year as his hitting progressed. Fielding was no problem for Radar. McMillan began 1951 in Tulsa, which had a Class AA team, and then was moved up to the majors partway through the same season. He played mostly at short but also some second and third base as a rookie. His hitting wasn't much (only .211) but the Reds weren't that concerned.

In fact, before they were more than a few games into the 1952 season, the Reds traded away their 1951 starting shortstop, Virgil Stallcup, and installed McMillan in the position. McMillan started every game for the Reds in 1952.

The fact that Stallcup had been the National League's leading shortstop in fielding and a .251 hitter showed what the Reds thought of their fledgling 21-year-old prospect, who was still learning the game.

The Reds stayed with McMillan despite his rocky start at bat, when he got only two hits in 52 at-bats. He justified their confidence by winding up the season with a decent .244 average. Lacking size, he still placed enough good hits to finish second on the team in runs-batted-in.

Typical of the play that kept him in the majors in those early years was a doubleheader in early 1952 against the Phillies.

In the first game, McMillan snared a line drive off hard-hitting Smokey Burgess, who could only shake his head in disbelief. Later McMillan dug a slow roller out of the ground and, off balance, threw long and hard to first base to beat out speedy Granny Hamner.

In the second game, McMillan hit his first homerun of the year. His next heroics were in the field. Radar got a grounder in back of second base and tossed out Richie Ashburn, one of the fastest runners in baseball, before he got to first. McMillan made the grab and the throw in one motion.

Thus, in less than six years after he played his first game of baseball, Roy McMillan was the best shortstop in the majors. McMillan lasted for 16 years in the majors, playing over 2,000 games at shortstop for the Reds, the Milwaukee Braves and the New York Mets.

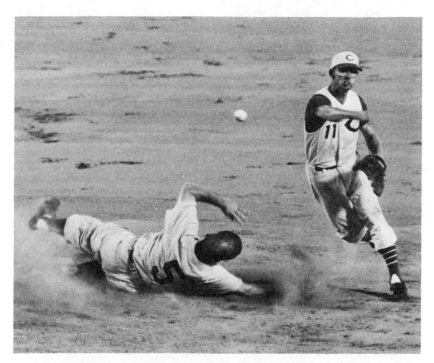

Roy McMillan made the jump from softball to baseball as effortlessly as he turned a double play.

Another player reached the major leagues in 1951—the same year as McMillan did—and shared the distinction of getting a big-league contract before he played his first baseball game.

But the circumstances were different for Eddie Gaedel.

Gaedel, who couldn't field a lick and never got the bat off his shoulder in his only appearance at the plate, was banned from baseball after just one at-bat. He was a midget, 43 inches (3 feet, 7 inches) "tall."

Gaedel's appearance for the St. Louis Browns in an

The St. Louis Browns reached a new "low" when they sent Eddie Gaedel to the plate.

official American League game against the Detroit Tigers on August 19, 1951, was something of a gimmick. When Gaedel waddled out of the Browns' dugout during the second game of a doubleheader between two teams going nowhere in the pennant race, umpire Ed Hurley challenged him. A man has to have a *bona fide* professional baseball contract, filed with the commissioner's office, before he can participate in a big-league game.

Gaedel reached into a pocket of his tailor-made Brown uniform, which bore the number "⅛", and showed Hurley what he didn't want to see—an official contract okayed by the major league office. Since it had been late in the season when several teams were bringing up unknown minor-league prospects, Gaedel's name was okayed at the commissioner's desk without a challenge. The whole event had been staged by Browns' owner Bill Veeck, as humorous an impresario as baseball has ever known. Veeck guarded his secret from just about everyone, including the people in his own organization.

He had hired Gaedel out of a circus and instructed him under threat of his life not to swing at any pitches once he got to bat against the Tigers.

The Tiger pitcher, Bob Cain, was so stunned in trying to put a ball into Gaedel's minuscule strike zone that he finally got down on his knees and pitched to the midget. But it was all in vain for Cain. Gaedel drew four straight balls and waddled down to first base, where he was quickly replaced with a pinch runner. Veeck had had his fun and just about everybody but the commissioner's office had a good laugh.

The next day, 26-year-old Eddie Gaedel was banned from baseball.

Playing for Different Teams

Pitcher Louis (Bobo) Newsom, the lovable loser, spent 25 years shuttling in and out of baseball cities, mostly in the majors.

Newsom pitched for "only" 18 *different* teams. But consider this. He was traded or sold to the Washington Senators four different times, the St. Louis Browns three times, and returned to the Brooklyn Dodgers—his initial big-league club in 1929—13 years later. Bobo played for nine different major-league teams. In addition, he also toiled for New York, Detroit, Boston and

Bobo Newsom was a pitcher who wore 18 different uniforms.

Philadelphia in the American League and New York and Chicago in the National. He was involved in trades that totaled 19 players.

Released outright by five different clubs in his later years, each time Newsom hooked up with another big-league club.

A 6-foot-3-inch 205-pounder, Newsom left some remarkable marks for losers to shoot for. He is, for instance, the only 20th Century 200-game winner to lose more than he won (211-222). He led the American League in losses a total of four times, a record. In 1938, he set a major-league record by giving up the most earned runs in a season—186—but still posted a 20-16 record for the St. Louis Browns.

But he probably reached his "peak" on September 18, 1934, when he pitched nine hitless innings for the Browns—but lost to the Boston Red Sox in the tenth inning!

*　　　*　　　*

Bobo Newsom probably would have been proud of Ted Gray, a fellow American League pitcher who hung around for nine years in the majors despite a losing record (59-74). In the left-hander's final season, 1955, Gray tied a big-league record by playing for four teams in the same season.

Gray did it the easy way: he played two games for the Chicago White Sox, two for the Cleveland Indians, one for the New York Yankees and finally nine for the Baltimore Orioles before calling it a career. That gave him four teams in just 19 games in one season—a tough act to follow. In all, he pitched only 23 innings.

The all-time record is held by Chester Covington, who was a late starter in professional baseball. He didn't pitch for money until he was 28. Seems that his other interests—he was a pro boxer, a patent medicine salesman, a railroad worker and a wrestling referee, among other things—absorbed his time until 1939 when he signed his first minor-league baseball contract.

Covington had been a man on the move before he joined the Portsmouth, Va., team, but it was nothing compared to the way he zigzagged through organized baseball. Covington played for a total of 21 different teams in the 12 years that were to follow his late debut. Counting repeat performances in some minor-league towns—and Tampa three times—Covington had 24 different assignments during his dozen years.

A rugged 225-pound left-hander, who had a 187-19-10 record as a boxer, Covington used to say he liked to train on "franks and beers." However he trained, he trained well. He had a total of 219 victories during his professional baseball career.

Though he joked around, he was no clown on the field. Two years after he signed his first contract, he ran up a 14-game winning streak. Two years later, in 1943, he was named Minor League Player of the Year for his performance with Scranton, Pa., of the Eastern League. Scranton was the tenth team Covington played for; so by then he had an opportunity to get some revenge on some of the teams that discarded him. In one of those moments, he tossed a perfect game against Springfield, Mass., with whom he had played a couple of years before. He stretched his string to 16⅔ hitless and 45 scoreless innings.

The good 1943 season earned Covington a trip to the majors for 1944. He pitched briefly, splitting a pair of decisions for the Philadelphia Phillies and getting thoroughly disgusted with management when he was forced to walk Stan Musial intentionally in one game.

Before the season was over, Covington was back in the minors with Utica, N.Y., to continue his minor-league odyssey. He was 34 at the time, but some of his best pitching was ahead of him.

In pitching for the Tampa Smokers in 1946, Covington displayed some remarkable control by walking only 55 men in 303 innings. In 1950, at age 39, he won 18 games for a second-division Fort Lauderdale club.

After that stopover, Covington moved to Tampa for the third time, then Lakeland, Fla., who dealt him to Sanford in the Florida State League. But for once, Covington declined an assignment. He joined the Greensboro team instead and posted a part-time 9-1 record, not bad for a 40-year-old.

One-Armed Outfielder

The talent in major-league baseball was thin in 1945. The more athletic Americans were overseas, trying to wind down World War II. Perhaps only in such an era could the big-league ranks include a one-armed outfielder. But for that one season, such a man earned publicity that would have made some Hall of Famers envious.

Pete (One-Arm) Gray was his name. And if the gutsy, little man was an oddity for the big leagues, he wasn't odd as a ballplayer. He came up through the minor leagues legitimately, and he stayed with the St. Louis Browns of the American League for a whole pennant-chasing season. Gray was good enough to be in a total of 77 major-league games that year, and more often than not he was entrusted to take an outfield position. "He's no side-show freak," maintained the Browns' manager, Luke Sewell. "He's a fine player, fast, courageous, and he can hit. We use him when he can help us win, the same as any two-armed player."

Born Peter J. Wyshner, he lost his arm at the age of six, when he fell off a truck and got it caught in the spokes of a wheel. When he had healed, he refused to let himself be denied sports. He played football, softball, basketball, hockey and other sports that were popular in the coal-mining town of Nanticoke, Pa. He put in such long hours at his games, especially baseball, that his father would end up delivering sandwiches to the playground to ensure that the boy got some nourishment. For hours, Pete would go off on his own and practice. He used to toss up rocks and hit them with a stick down near the railroad yards. Before long, his left wrist became very powerful.

Young Wyshner changed his name to Pete Gray after his brother adopted that last name during a prizefighting career. Then the new Pete Gray set out to make a living professionally in sports, too. His hard work paid off for him by the time he was 16. Though he didn't play high-school baseball, he was better than the other sandlotters in the coal-mining area. He was confident, too.

In 1939, Pete went to the World's Fair in New York City. He brought his glove along, because he had heard that baseball tryouts were being held in Brooklyn. Pete didn't connect with any team that year, but three seasons later, at age 25, he hooked up with the Three Rivers, Ont., team in the Canadian-American League. Despite a broken collarbone in his debut, Gray made a comeback and batted .381.

Quickly he was promoted to the Memphis Chicks

For Pete Gray, playing baseball with only one arm came natural to him.

team of the Southern Association. He began to make a name for himself, hitting .289 in 1943 and .333 the following year. During that banner 1944 campaign, Pete was a terror on the basepaths, stealing 68 times (including 10 thefts of home plate).

For those who figured his one arm would prove to be too much of a handicap in the outfield, Pete had a surprise. He fielded well, catching the ball in his specially made glove with no padding, then quickly tucking the glove under the stump of his right arm, digging out the ball and throwing it—all in one effortless motion. In one game, Pete made an unassisted double play from centerfield.

At the end of the 1944 season, 14 of the Southern Association's top sportswriters sent in their ballots for the league's Most Valuable Player. Gray's name topped the list on 12 of them.

The St. Louis Browns, who had just won the American League pennant, paid Memphis $20,000 for Gray's contract and offered the amazing one-armed player an opportunity to make the big leagues.

After a slow start in spring training, in which he had only a drag bunt hit to show for 13 at-bats, Gray went 4-for-9 and scored three runs in two games. That, coupled with his flawless fielding (10 putouts, one assist, no errors in five games) enabled him to make the Brown team.

Once the regular season began, the 28-year-old rookie proved he was big-league caliber even though he was no day-to-day star.

The Browns were paying for talent, but they soon found out they had acquired a drawing card, too. At a time when baseball was suffering from wartime doldrums, huge crowds flocked to see Pete Gray wherever he traveled in the American League. Once 65,000 turned out to see him play at Cleveland. Pete treated the curiosity seekers to a triple on his first time up. A like number of fans were expected to see him play for the first time at Yankee Stadium, but a bad-weather forecast dampened the enthusiasm. Still, 40,000 fans braved the weather. Pete was giving the big leagues a much-needed shot in the arm.

The Browns often took advantage of Gray's appeal. In the Yankee Stadium debut, Manager Sewell purposely held him back during the pregame introduction of the Brown players. When Pete finally took the field, he got a standing ovation.

His popularity caused some alarm among teammates, who were envious of his unintentional wooing of the crowds. They sometimes felt he was put in games ahead of better players just to satisfy the fans. And umpires were perturbed that Gray could do no wrong in the eyes of the crowds, whether they were Brown fans or not.

But Gray often held his own, playing against such standouts as Bobby Feller and Hal Newhouser.

He earned most of his plaudits. In an important series with the New York Yankees early in the season, Pete displayed his prowess both at bat and in the field. He singled twice in the first inning of a crucial doubleheader and was the focal point of a Brown rally for seven runs. He singled again in the third and drove in a run in the fifth as the Browns won the opener, 10-1. During that same game, he went back to the leftfield wall for important putouts, one with the bases loaded and two outs.

In the nightcap, Gray walked, singled and also came within a half-step of beating out a drag bunt. In the outfield, he made six putouts, including a line-drive catch that he snared below his knees while on a dead run. The Browns won that game, too. A crowd of more than 20,000 showered him with applause all afternoon.

Later in the season, during a July 4 twin bill against the Philadelphia Athletics, Gray's 32-ounce bat exploded again. He slugged a long double and two singles against the A's best pitcher and drove in the winning runs in the process.

Pete's play inspired a St. Louis baseball reporter to write, "It was a great exhibition of courage and you can use that word without restraint or blush, even in these war-torn days, when you sing of a gamester like Peter Gray."

Gray got into 77 games during the 1945 season, mostly as a regular outfielder. Crowds poured into once-empty stadiums even when it was unlikely that he would play. Sometimes, his appearances—demanded by the curious fans—worked against the Browns' efforts to defend their American League title. In a game against the Yankees, for example, the Browns had an 8-2 lead in the last of the seventh inning, so Manager Sewell decided to treat the 40,000-strong crowd to a look at Gray. Pete fumbled a single during a Yankee rally and the Browns subsequently lost the game in extra innings—and also the second game of the doubleheader. The Browns never did recover from that twin loss and finished in third place.

For the entire season, Pete only batted .218. That, coupled with the return of baseball veterans from the war in 1946, shortened Gray's big-league career. In November, 1945, his contract was sold to Toledo of the American Association.

Even Pete admitted, "The pitching is a little bit too tough for me up there (in the majors)."

He shipped out to Toledo for 1946, dropped a few notches on the minor-league scale to Elmira, N.Y., for 1948, then moved upward again to Dallas in 1949 before finally retiring. But the stint in the majors earned Pete his share of immortality, to say nothing of a little extra cash. Parlaying his fame in the off-season one fall, he earned $5,400 on a short barnstorming tour.

*   *   *

Pete Gray wasn't the only one-armed player to compete at the major-league level. On September 13, 1883, Hugh Dailey of the Cleveland team in the National League had hurled a no-hitter against the Philadelphia ballclub and came out a 1-0 winner. "One-Arm" Dailey also pitched 18 other shutouts during his big-league career with eight teams in the 1880s, and totaled 74 victories in all.

Scoring after the Last Out

On May 28, 1922, a 2-1 duel between the New York Yankees and the St. Louis Browns seemed to be over, with the powerful Yankees winning as usual. Yank pitcher Sam Jones, who had been hit freely but fruitlessly by the Browns, retired the first two Browns to face him in the ninth inning before an overflow, boisterous crowd in New York. Then two Browns reached base with singles. After the next batter, John Tobin, hit a slow roller to the first baseman, Jones headed toward first to cover that base. The Brown baserunner who had been on second base went all the way home. As Jones took the underhand throw for the third out, the fans spilled onto the field and chased the players to their dressing rooms.

But then the umpire reversed himself and ruled that Jones had juggled the catch at first base, making Tobin safe, and making the score 2-all with the game unfinished.

Within fifteen minutes, the players were recalled to the field, the diamond was cleaned up and the fans were shooed back in the stands. One player was summoned out of the shower.

Tobin, who had scored the Browns' only other run in the eighth inning when the Yankees had a 2-0 lead, went to first base.

From then on in, what should have been a routine victory for the Yanks, who were winning regularly despite the suspension of Babe Ruth, turned into a nightmare.

When play resumed the first man up singled, driving in the go-ahead run for the Browns. The next batter was walked intentionally to fill the bases, but the Yankees were getting madder and madder by the moment. Particularly the pitcher.

He walked the next man and forced Tobin in.

Then a Brown cleaned the bases with a homerun. And Urban Shocker, the ace of the St. Louis staff, put the embarrassed Yanks down in order in the bottom of the ninth.

The Browns had scored seven runs on the Yanks after the "last out." They won 8-2, when they should have been back at their hotel moaning a defeat.

The game was significant for the upstart Browns, who weren't considered in the same class with the Yankees. But St. Louis battled the New Yorkers down to the final game before losing the pennant that season.

Unusual Twinbill

When the Milwaukee Braves prepared for a double-header on September 24, 1954, the scouting report before the game was bigger than usual. That day the Braves would have to play two different teams.

It happened this way:

Two days earlier, the Braves had met the Cincinnati Reds for what seemed to be the final match between the two teams during the regular season. The Braves won, 3-1, but the Reds protested a play.

The Reds had been trailing 3-1 in the ninth inning with one out and runners on first and third. Cincy's Bob Borkowski struck out, but Braves catcher Del Crandall couldn't hold onto the ball, so Borkowski dashed to first.

Meanwhile, Crandall picked up the ball and threw to third baseman Eddie Mathews, who missed tagging the runner, Gus Bell, and quickly tossed to first to try to get Borkowski. The ball hit the baserunner on the back and bounced into rightfield. Two runners scored, tying the game. But after a 15-minute dispute, the Braves were awarded the victory.

Then National League President Warren Giles upheld Cincinnati's protest. With the season coming to a close and the Braves involved in the pennant race, Cincinnati was ordered to go back to Milwaukee on September 24 for the finish of the disputed game. The September 22nd game was replayed with Bell at third and a man at second, which was consistent with Giles' ruling. The score was held at 3-1, Milwaukee's favor, and two outs.

After the game was started again, Cincinnati got two runs and tied the score at 3-all. But the Braves scored in the bottom of the ninth and won, 4-3.

Meanwhile, the St. Louis Cardinals were watching all this, waiting to play their own previously scheduled September 24 date with the Braves.

The Braves took that contest, too, by a 4-2 score.

It was all academic, though. Neither the Braves, nor the Cards, nor the Reds got to go to the World Series.

The 26-Inning Game

It rained in Boston on the morning of May 1, 1920. What players and fans had hoped would be a sunny May Day dampened their enthusiasm for the scheduled 3 o'clock game between the hometown Braves and the visiting Brooklyn Dodgers. The players had to show up, however, when it was announced that the game would be played as scheduled. A small crowd of 2,000 turned out.

Too bad. The pitchers, Brooklyn's Leon Cadore and Boston's Joe Oeschger, had staged an 11-inning, 1-0 duel when they had met two weeks previously. The Dodgers won that one.

But it was too bad for other reasons, too. For Cadore and Oeschger were about to turn in one of the greatest "iron men" feats on record.

The game began rather routinely, with neither team scoring until the fifth inning. Then the Dodgers scored, when Cadore advanced a runner into scoring position with a fielder's choice play and Ivan Olson singled the man home.

The Braves tied the score in the sixth inning after Wally Cruise tripled with one man out, and scored on a single. Actually, the Dodgers could have nailed Cruise when he took off for home after a short fly to leftfield. Brooklyn's Zack Wheat made a shoestring catch of the ball and tried to double Cruise, who had run halfway to the plate. But there was no fielder on third to take the throw. Cruise scampered back to the bag safely and later scored on the single.

It was the end of the scoring—but hardly the end of the game. For 20 more innings, one goose egg after another was entered into the box score. Two baseball teams played exceedingly tight defense and refused to allow a run.

There were a few threats, like the Braves' rally in the ninth when they filled the bases only to get caught in a double play. The Dodgers made a bid to win in the 17th inning only to have an amazing double play (pitcher to catcher to first to catcher) stymie the rally. The throw to first had not been on time but the first baseman, Walt Holke, got it home in time to stop the would-be scorer. It was Holke's only assist of the day but next to the pitchers he got the biggest workout that May Day. He made a total of 42 putouts at first, and didn't have an error.

Batters came up short in both lineups. But other than Charley Pick, the Braves' second baseman (0-for-11), Cadore (0-for-10) and the Dodgers shortstop, Chuck Ward, who was likewise collared in 10 trips to the plate, 12 of the 15 who played the entire game got at least one hit each.

Rabbit Maranville, the Braves' shortstop, and Tony Boeckel, the Braves' third baseman, were the top hitters of the marathon, each going 3-for-10.

For the Dodgers, Jimmy Johnston, the third baseman, and Wheat, the leftfielder, led the non-attack with two hits apiece. Perhaps it was justice that Maranville and Wheat came through, for they were the only future Hall of Famers in the game.

The real heroes, however, were pitchers Oeschger of Boston and Cadore of Brooklyn. They went all the way—26 innings in baseball's longest game, inning-wise.

Oeschger gave up just nine hits in pitching the equivalent of nearly three full games. Cadore gave up only 15 hits. They each struck out just seven men, but they walked only nine players between them.

Oeschger had gotten the Sunday starting assignment because his manager, George Stallings, was a superstitious type who figured his religious, church-going right-hander might get a few breaks from the Man Upstairs if he pitched on the Sabbath. As it turned out, the Man was treating everybody the same—very evenly, to be sure—that May 1, 1920. After 26 innings—spanning 3 hours and 50 minutes—of baseball, the game was called.

The players were begging for an additional inning. They wanted to be able to say that they had played three full games within one. But it was getting too dark to continue. Umpire Barry McCormick told them they'd have to wear miners' lamps on their baseball caps if they wanted to go on.

Pitcher Cadore was one of the biggest protesters. But after the game was called, he justified the umpire's decision when he went home and slept for 36 straight hours. Meanwhile, Oeschger had to contend with stories in Boston papers that his career was probably ruined by the 26-inning marathon. He squelched that talk by pitching, and winning, eight days later.

The game was finally played off on June 25, with Boston winning. But the finish has been obscured by history. What was historically important was a pitching duel and a tight defense in baseball's longest game.

*　　　　*　　　　*

There have been games that took more time. Marathon games of more than 6½ hours have been played in the majors, particularly in the 1960s. For short-term games, one must go back into history. The New York Giants beat the Philadelphia Phillies, 6-1, in a 51-minute nine-inning game in 1919.

But the real quickie must have been the showdown on August 30, 1916, between the Asheville and Winston-Salem teams in the North Carolina League.

The minor leaguers were playing an unimportant late-season contest that day, and since they traveled by train the visiting Winston-Salem manager requested a fast match. The starting time of the game was moved up from 2 P.M. to 1:28. By 1:59—31 minutes later—the two teams had their nine innings in.

The hitters swung at everything that was pitched and tried particularly to connect on first pitches. The teams raced to their positions when in the field, and on one occasion they almost resumed play without a catcher. The game moved along so fast that the regular umpire was stunned to learn that four innings had passed by the time he arrived on the scene slightly ahead of time for the scheduled 2 o'clock start.

Somehow the teams found the time to score three runs between them. Winston-Salem won the game, 2-1, before dashing off to catch the 3 o'clock train.

Streaking to Nowhere

Early in the season, tough-minded John McGraw felt that his 1916 New York Giants were spending too much effort trying to break the major-league record of 19 straight victories. So he tore his club apart halfway through the campaign. Despite the fact that the Giants had won 17 straight and had come close to matching the 19 in a row racked up by the 1906 Chicago White Sox, McGraw didn't hesitate when the streak came to an end and the team slumped into playing .500 ball. He discarded two of his best veterans and demoted his catcher. McGraw was that way: today's game was more important than yesterday's history.

Gone were Larry Doyle, one of the finest second basemen McGraw ever had, and Bill McKechnie, a competent third baseman. McGraw brought in Buck Herzog for second and Heinie Zimmerman for third. He also acquired Lew McCarthy from the league-leading Brooklyn Dodgers to handle the catching when he became disenchanted with the incumbents at that position. Herzog, Zimmerman and McCarthy were all major-league veterans.

The Giants weren't about to catch the high-flying Dodgers but the fearful McGraw apparently affected them with his wholesale shake-up of the ballclub.

After the Giants split a doubleheader with the Dodgers on September 6, losing the second game, little Ferdie Schupp, a rookie McGraw wanted to see more of, tossed a two-hitter against the Dodgers. He won the game, 4-1. The next day, Jeff Tesreau outdueled the great Grover Cleveland Alexander of the Philadelphia Phillies.

Giant fans began coming alive now that their new-look team was pulling together. In fact, 35,000 of them showed up for a September 9 doubleheader—the largest crowd up to that time to witness a game at the Polo Grounds.

Pol Perritt gave the crowd something more to cheer about. Pitching both ends of the doubleheader against the Phillies, Perritt gave up only eight hits and one run.

He collected a pair of 3-1 and 3-0 triumphs for his iron-man efforts.

After a day off, the Giants continued to win day in and day out. They beat the Phillies again and swept four straight games from the Cincinnati Reds.

With Schupp, Tesreau and Rube Benton pitching magnificently, McCarthy hitting nearly .400 and the new infielders blending in, the Giants became unstoppable. There was a temporary snag after they won 12 straight games. On September 18, after they beat the Pittsburgh Pirates in the first half of a doubleheader, the second game was called in the ninth inning because of darkness. The Giants and Pirates were tied 1-1 at the time. But ties don't figure in winning streaks.

The Giants picked up where they left off by sweeping the Pirates in another doubleheader the next day. Then Schupp, with just a day's rest, defeated the Chicago Cubs, 4-2.

With the season coming to a close and the Giants going nowhere in the standing, it suddenly dawned upon them that they were going to get a second chance at matching the White Sox' record of 19 straight victories.

Slim Salee, a curveball artist who had missed several weeks of action due to illness, came off the sick list to pitch the Giants to their 17th straight when he blanked the Chicago Cubs. Then the Giants matched the White Sox major league record of 19 with a sweep of the St. Louis Cardinals on September 23.

The rash of late-season doubleheaders seemed to increase the probability of defeat. But not for the Giants, who were breathing new life into a lost season. After a day off, they swept the Cards in yet another twinbill. It was their seventh doubleheader in September, and they had only the tie with the Pirates to mar their slate.

The Cards came close to snapping the streak at 22 games when they took a 2-0 lead into the ninth inning. But the Giants came back to tie the game and win it in the tenth on Zimmerman's base running. Zimmerman opened the tenth with a single, moved to second and third on back-to-back bunts, then scored on a wild pitch.

Next opponents were the Boston Braves. Tesreau and Schupp teamed up in a doubleheader to sweep the Braves as each recorded his sixth pitching victory of the streak, which had now reached 25 games. A rain-out the following day forced the weary Giants into another doubleheader with the Braves.

Rube Benton became the third Giant pitcher to reach six victories during the streak in the opening game on September 30. And he pitched better than any Giant yet. Benton faced only 28 batters as he won, 4-0. A single by Ed Konetchy ruined Benton's hopes for a perfect game.

The Giants had now won seven doubleheaders and 26 straight games—nine of them by shutouts. Only five times had an opponent come as close as one run.

Rest was a premium the Giants had forgotten about. Between September 7, when the streak began, and September 30, they had only three Sundays off. They were rained out two other days, and had to come right back and make up those games. The Giants had beaten every team in the league and shut out all of them except the Dodgers at least once.

But in the second game of the September 30 doubleheader, luck ran out. The Braves crushed the Giants, 8-3.

No team has come close to matching the Giant streak of 26 in that 1916 season. The 1935 Chicago Cubs strung together 21 games in a pennant-winning year. The 1947 New York Yankees won 19 in a row.

To add a fillip to their record, the Giants had won all 26 games at home—a feat almost impossible to match. (In their original streak that year, they had won all 17 games on the road.)

Yet for all their efforts, the 1916 Giants could finish no better than fourth place, seven games behind the league-leading Brooklyn Dodgers.

Percentage Games

As terrific as Dwight Gooden and Roger Clemens were in the mid-1980s, they still couldn't break into one list of baseball's all-time greats. That is the category for pitchers with the most victories per defeat.

Here is a list of that top 10:

Losses	Wins	Pitcher, Team, Year	Pct.
0	12	Tom Zachary, N.Y. Yankees, 1929	1.000
1	18	El Roy Face, Pittsburgh Pirates, 1959	.947
2	16	Freddie Fitzsimmons, Brooklyn Dodgers, 1940	.889
3	25	Ron Guidry, N.Y. Yankees, 1978	.893
4	31	Lefty Grove, Phila. Athletics, 1931	.886
5	34	Joe Wood, Boston Red Sox, 1912	.872
6	31	Dennis McLain, Detroit Tigers, 1968	.838
7	36	Walter Johnson, Wash. Senators, 1913	.837
8	35	Joe McGinnity, N.Y. Giants, 1904	.814
9	31	Jack Coombs, Phila. Athletics, 1910	.775
10	33	Cy Young, Boston Red Sox, 1901	.767

Departures from games were never quiet events for Earl Weaver.

You're Out

Earl Weaver made a name for himself in 17 years of managing the Baltimore Orioles before stepping down from the job after the 1986 season. In all, he managed in more than 2,500 regular-season games, and he managed in four post-season playoffs and four World Series.

He also made a name for himself with umpires: on 98 occasions (believed to be a record), he managed to get himself thrown out of the game.

Roster of Players